Get more from work
– and more fun

Neasa MacErlean is a business journalist on the *Observer*, where she started the 'How to . . .' column in 1995. She read English at Reading University and qualified as a chartered accountant before entering journalism in 1986. She has at different times worked as a fiction reviewer, features writer and general news reporter. But she believes the best experience she gained for these columns was her various casual jobs as a waitress, filing clerk and cleaner. She lives in North London.

To Ruth Dudley Edwards: friend, mentor, example and aunt

Get more from work
– *and more fun*

Neasa MacErlean

INSTITUTE OF PERSONNEL AND DEVELOPMENT

Typesetting by Wyvern 21, Bristol
and printed in Great Britain by
the Cromwell Press, Trowbridge, Wiltshire

British Library Cataloguing in Publication Data
A catalogue record for this book is available from the British Library

ISBN 0-85292-750-9

IPD House, Camp Road, Wimbledon, London SW19 4UX
Tel: 0181-971-9000   Fax: 0181-263-3333
Registered office as above. Registered Charity No. 1038333
A company limited by guarantee. Registered in England No. 2931892

Contents

Improving communications

Redundancy, being sacked . . . and starting again

Useful addresses and telephone numbers   209

Acknowledgements

One of the great pleasures of writing this book has been to draw on the good nature and help of a wide range of colleagues and experts, many of whom became friends in the process. Many friends were also pressed into service.

I want to thank Tahmina Ashraf and Abigail Sanderson for running an administrative powerhouse with endless good humour. Many thanks also to my *Observer* colleagues Ben Laurance and Maria Scott for their encouragement – and for being the very models of modern managers. I relied on the expertise and lively views of several experts – including Jo Bond, Michael Burd, Michael Carroll, Melissa Compton-Edwards, James Davies, Memuna Forna, Paul Le Druillenec and Frances Wilks. Patrick Cosgrave and Ruth Dudley Edwards taught me how to write. Friendly criticism and moral support came from Bob Brodie, Peter Carty, Shirley Cosgrave, David Cresswell, Caroline Dawnay, Peter Day, Patrick Dudley Edwards, the late Sheila Durston, David Evans, Jill Fornary, Nick Gillies, Zoe Hayes, Sylvia Kalisch, Gary Kent, John Mattock, Eoin O'Neachtain, Margot Sreberny and David Webb.

This book would not have been written without the ceaseless encouragement and kindness of Brendan Donnelly MEP.

Introduction

The workplace abounds with people who are paid very well for doing their jobs badly. It also includes many people – probably several million – who are severely underpaid for performing their duties magnificently. Anyone who wants to get their just rewards (or better) needs to understand their rights and to fight their corner. This book aims to tell you how to do that – not just in relation to pay and conditions, but also as regards job satisfaction, career development and relationships with colleagues and contacts.

Why the workplace is a jungle

After thousands of years employing one another, human beings still tend to reward good marketing over genuine ability in the workplace. Selling yourself to the right people at the right time is often a far more important factor in success than being genuinely good at your job. It is relatively rare to find someone truly outstanding at the top of their tree. Even in sports jobs, where people's abilities are fairly easy to measure, disastrous appointments are often made. England cricket captains (until recently) have largely been disappointing since the golden days of Mike Brearley in the 1970s and 1980s. Managers of Arsenal

Football Club lacked the elusive touch to win 'the double' for 27 years until an outsider and relative unknown, Arsène Wenger, arrived at Highbury and the team came top of the league and won the FA Cup in 1998.

It is not just at the top that one finds mediocre individuals. The operation of the workplace often gives safe harbour to huge swathes of unproductive and inefficient workers. In developed countries, lawyers are seen as the great example of people who are overpaid for the work they do. In the UK, the highest-flying young solicitors could earn £28,000 in 1998, nearly 50 per cent more than the average wage. But many lawyers have huge patches of incompetence. In fact, the English solicitors' profession had received so many negligence claims by 1998 that the total bill amounted to £17,000 per partner in every law firm.

Another UK example is provided by the professionals at Lloyd's of London who made a fortune for themselves in the 1980s while giving their clients ('Names') such poor advice that many went bankrupt and some committed suicide. Then there is the best-paying sector (as defined by the Office of National Statistics) – financial services – where the average salary of everyone working in the field approached £26,000 in 1998. Thousands of people in this field became rich in the early 1990s by mis-selling personal pensions to relatively poorly paid nurses, teachers, miners and other workers. They got rewarded for being not just bad at their jobs but also unscrupulous.

At the other end of the spectrum are secretaries and nannies, both consistently underpaid for their demanding duties. Very few of the country's 800,000 secretaries earn more than £25,000 – despite the fact that many have become the office *éminences grises* in the 1990s by mastering information technology skills. And the average childcare worker earns less than £9,000 (not quite half the average wage), despite the long hours and huge responsibilities.

So what sorts out the sheep from the goats, the undeserving and well-remunerated from the deserving and poor? One overriding factor. The undeserving appreciate that the workplace is not a market that systematically rewards virtue – and they play their cards accordingly.

Why conscientious workers lose out

People who are genuinely good at their work make two common errors. First, they often take such pride in doing the job well that they neglect to market themselves. In fact, there is frequently a correlation between huge talent and a lack of worldliness. The people who make the great creative advances are not always the ones who end up rich. Sir Barnes Wallis, inventor of the bouncing bomb, which was part of the crucial effort to destroy the German industrial heartlands in the Second World War, ended his life living in fair comfort but was certainly not wealthy. Henry Ford made a fortune from the motor car, but he was not the person who invented it.

Secondly, there has been a tendency among UK workers to accept their lot without question. Even the most intelligent people have worked for years in jobs they hated and each day carried out instructions they disagreed with. Thousands of miners protested at the closure of the pits in the early 1990s even though mining twisted their backs, gave them emphysema and left them covered in coal and dirt (lack of alternative employment was obviously a factor, but far from the whole story). Generations of workers have passed on to each other a high degree of willingness to conform.

This reflects the origins of the workplace – the military structure that shapes our lives even today. We may not realise it, but many of us still work in organisations that are fundamentally modelled on the army. For example, many employees are required to start work punctually at a very particular time, often 9.00 or 9.30am. In many companies, there is no longer a rationale for this: it is merely a throwback to the way battles used to start. Ringing a bell or blowing a trumpet at an arranged time was the only way to organise hundreds of men in the days before modern technology. Similarly, millions of employees wear a uniform – another necessity in battles, but of declining relevance for most parts of today's workforce. The very layout of desks in offices used to reflect a battle formation. But the huge anonymous halls that characterised 1950s offices – where rank after rank of employees sat facing in the same direction at identical desks – have largely disappeared, to be replaced by cosier, more individual arrangements. Nevertheless, the very idea of leadership in a business context has often been closely modelled on military leadership. Until the 1980s, most large companies had a rigid hierarchical structure presided over by bosses whose orders were merely to be obeyed, never to be questioned. Some organisations are still like that. But many of the more successful ones have gradually moved away from these military influences – even though they probably did not realise that this was what they were doing.

In the past, most workers had little option but to conform – rather like soldiers. Rigid dress codes (blue-collar workers, white-collar workers, a ban on trousers for women in most occupations . . .) were an outward reflection of the discipline required of most employees.

But in the 1990s the world changed dramatically (mirrored, incidentally, for many employees in a relaxation of the unspoken rules covering workplace dress). The end of 'the job for life' meant that people had to start thinking for themselves. Until then, employees needed to conform so that they could hold on to their jobs. Now they need to differentiate themselves so that they can get the next one.

The new millennium – a new start in the workplace

The last years of the old millennium have transformed the world of work in many ways:

- The 1997 election of the Labour government saw a sea change in political attitudes to employment. Through its 'welfare to work' programmes for the unemployed, disabled and lone parents, the government made clear that work is intended to be the passport to self-respect in the new world.

- Workers were given basic rights they had never had before – including the right to paid holiday; the right to work fewer than 48 hours a week; and the right to paternity leave. Most spectacular was the right to a minimum wage, for the first time covering the whole workforce, in 1999. With Margaret Beckett presiding as Labour's first

Secretary of State at the Department of Trade and Industry, the Blair government was influenced by much more left-wing views on the rights of workers than is generally appreciated.

- Parts of a fundamentally different employment infrastructure are being imported from the Continent. Most European Union workplace legislation has been profoundly benign for workers. Health and safety procedures have been systematically improved under its influence. German ideas of a partnership between workers and bosses have started to find their way to the UK. Workers now have much greater rights to consultation, for example – on the future of the company as a whole and on particular areas such as redundancies.

- Job insecurity has become a way of life. Even in the booming days of the late 1990s, about 800,000 people a year (one in 30 workers) were being made redundant. Few people now expect a long-term job. Most will have experience of redundancy, casual employment, part-time jobs, and contract or freelance work.

- Continuous learning and training are emerging as the best way to cope with job insecurity. If you cannot hold on to a job for ever, you can still make yourself employable for a long time by learning new skills. Good employers increasingly provide training for their staff. The government has set up the University for Industry. In the new millennium, more individuals will pay for their own training.

What further changes shall we see?

The UK government – like others in the developed world – will be forced to make two specific changes early in the new millennium:

- The retirement age will be increased to between 70 and 75. The fact that longevity is increasing by about two years each decade means that a retirement age of 65 is out of date. Now that women can expect to live to 80 and men to 75, they need to find something else to do with their retirement years than play bowls. Older people who want to live a comfortable life financially need to find it easier to get part-time work.
- Workers will be forced to make private provision for their pensions (and should be encouraged to invest at least 15 per cent of their income). Most politicians realise that this move is necessary, but think that it could take several years of public discussion before the electorate agrees with them. People who do not provide for their old age will lead very restricted lives after they retire.

How to read this book

This book is a guide to negotiating the pitfalls in today's workplace. It is divided into chapters that advise you on different aspects of the workplace and help you deal with the practical situations that constantly arise. Different people will read it in different ways. Someone starting work might read the first two chapters straight through. Someone losing their job could start with the last chapter. Others in work might dip into the book as particular issues affect them – as most will during the course of an average working life. The book was completed in summer 1998 and describes the law then. You will need to remember that the legal framework is changing all the time.

Chapter introductions

Getting started

The process of getting the right job is one of the most difficult hurdles you will encounter in your life. Traditional recruitment techniques are notoriously inadequate. Poor interviewers tend to choose people like themselves, and rarely pick candidates cleverer than themselves. Good companies try to compensate for these weaknesses by using several recruitment methods, for instance interviews, psychometric tests or open days. This makes the selection procedure more complicated and time-consuming, but also gives you a better chance to display your talents.

The problems are compounded for young people, who may not know what sort of job they want. In the past, the main problem was lack of choice. In the 1960s, a clever, middle-class girl would usually choose between nursing, teaching and secretarial work. Nowadays, there are 40,000 university courses to decide between before you even begin to think about employment. But people who plan carefully can give themselves a strong advantage in today's marketplace of over 27 million workers.

Pay and conditions

The amount you get paid usually depends on five main factors: the job you do, your qualifications for it, length of service, ability to negotiate and the location. If you want to get rich, avoid the low-paying sectors. Childcare, hairdressing, kitchen portering, waitressing and bar work are the worst-paying jobs, according to the Low Pay Unit. Qualifications are becoming increasingly important, although practical skills (notably in IT) are now more valued in some sectors than examination passes. Length of service is now a double-edged sword. When they 'downsize', many employers choose to get rid of their older, more expensive employees. The decline of the unions in the 1980s has put more pressure on individuals to negotiate their own pay. Location can be a surprisingly influential factor – unless you work for a national company with national pay scales. Pay is highest in the UK in the City of London, where the average annual salary was £37,000 in 1998. It is lowest in the Welsh town of Conwy and in Cornwall, where people earn just under £14,800 a year on average. But the arrival of new employers in town can have a dramatic effect on wages. Pay rose by 14 per cent in Swindon in 1997, largely as a result of increased demand for workers. Women tend to earn less than men do – typically 27 per cent less. Although the average male full-time annual salary was £21,000 in 1998, the average full-time female salary was £15,400.

Most employees make two errors that set them back at work. They do not understand their employment rights, and they do not appreciate benefits other than pay. Employers may break the law, wittingly and unwittingly – and could frequently be forced to pay compensation, if only their staff knew it. Similarly, employers have been able to cut back on the pensions and perks they provide, because few individuals understand how valuable those benefits are.

Becoming successful

The workplace is littered with people who are bad at their jobs but successful in getting promotion. A little bit of talent can get you a long way – if you play your cards right. Even very clever people can be weak in the wrong job. The appointment of the well-regarded criminal barrister Barbara Mills QC as Director of Public Prosecutions was widely seen as a mistake. She agreed to stand down in 1998, after an independent report ripped apart the cumbersome structures she had established in the previous six years at the Crown Prosecution Service. A less well-known example was the recruitment of leading accountant Elwyn Eilledge to chair industrial group BTR: after continued criticism, he also stood down in 1998. Like thousands before them, these two people were appointed because their faces fitted; there was insufficient consideration as to whether they could do the job.

One of the great historical examples of the rise of the undeserving was the promotion of the 7th Earl of Cardigan as a military leader in the Crimean War. Clearly incompetent, unable to understand the basics of providing food and shelter for his troops, he was chosen above dozens of men with far greater abilities. It was only when he led more than 500 men to their death in the disastrous Charge of the Light Brigade in 1854 that his weaknesses were finally recognised. He owed his promotion to a rigid class structure and to the fact that the people who chose him were also out of touch with modern warfare.

Today's workplace is far less hierarchical and less prejudiced. But good workers will still be passed over in favour of modern-day Cardigans, unless they work out their own strategies.

Overcoming difficulties

Nearly everyone will face some kind of catastrophe or crisis during their career. Your ability to handle this disaster could affect your reputation and shape your career for years afterwards. Conservative MP Ann Widdecombe became hugely respected after she felt compelled to criticise her former boss, Michael Howard. Some crises will be caused by you or those near you, rather than your work. In these cases – you realise you are drinking too much, for example – you may have to forget your pride and ask for help from your employer.

Reacting to change

Your ability to adapt to new circumstances will be your lifeline. Modern companies do not stand still. In a good company, you will constantly be acquiring new skills. In a more troubled environment, you may be taken over, see your colleagues made redundant, get a new boss or be asked to perform your job in a different way. Dramatic change is usually preceded by certain signs. If you know how to recognise them, you will give yourself a major head-start. People taken unawares are sometimes so shocked that they are unable to react quickly enough. Many people get fired because they are unable to be flexible.

Relating to other people

Most of us see our childhood and family as the great moulding influences on our characters. But adulthood and the workplace can have an even greater effect, if you decide to learn from your relations with colleagues. If you have a particular personality trait that you want to work on, you can rapidly get a lot of room for improvement at work. You think you are too shy, for instance – so practise initiating conversations in the coffee queue, or just with people in the corridor. For the 15 per cent of the UK population (over 8 million people) who live alone, human contact at work is even more important.

Most of us are happy to keep a clear dividing line between home life and work. Although you can afford to be grumpy with your family sometimes, you need to be consistently affable at work. But sometimes the two worlds interact – such as when, for instance, you become involved with someone at work.

Improving communications

Your popularity at work depends largely on one character trait: your ability to make other people feel good about themselves. This doesn't mean you have to toady to people: many of the most successful working relations are built on forthright communications. But you do need to respect other people – say hello and good-bye, listen to their views, thank them and be very careful about how you communicate information, particularly criticism. The days of the tyrannical boss are coming to end.

Understanding the characters

Most of the people you meet at work should be treated as individuals and not be stereotyped. But there are some people who are difficult to deal with – who have certain symptoms that it is useful to diagnose. The woman at the next desk to you may be kind and pleasant 95 per cent of the time, but then becomes angry or goes missing when you have deadlines to meet. She is, perhaps, a perfectionist who will always let you down when she is put under pressure. It is far better to realise this early on in your relationship.

Parties and other events

Parties are becoming more widespread as companies realise that staff well-being is good for the bottom line. This means that most employees will, at some point in the year, get free hospitality from their employers. But parties have their dangerous side. The Christmas bash is potentially the worst. The employment law team at solicitors Lewis Silkin estimates that 90 per cent of their post-party sexual harassment workload arrives in December and January. Staff are less likely to hit the bottle with such vigour at the summer barbecue or on the company outing to the greyhound races.

Research from the Industrial Society suggests that 54 per cent of women and 15 per cent of men have experienced unwanted sexual attentions at work. In the past, many people routinely put up with *Carry On*-style behaviour and presumably bit their lips as they were chased around the desk. But in the late 1990s, there has been considerable publicity on this subject. Even the unwanted avuncular hug can get people into trouble.

Sickness and stress

Employers are becoming more careful in the way they manage staff sickness. People who are regularly unwell without good reason are increasingly attracting the attention of the personnel department. But people still take off an average of eight days a year. As much as half of this is attributable to stress. Many people frightened of redundancy are working longer hours to try to safeguard their jobs. It can be a false economy. If you succumb to burnout, it may take a long time to recover.

Discipline

Going through disciplinary proceedings is usually the workplace equivalent of hearing your death-knell. Only one person in four makes an attempt to resume normal working life afterwards (according to research conducted at the University of Huddersfield) by deciding to change their behaviour in pursuit of rehabilitation. Most people believe that such treatment was meted out to them by superiors purely for personal reasons.

In the 1990s, some employers have started to see dismissal on disciplinary grounds as a cheap alternative to making redundancy payments. The banking union BIFU regularly defends members who are hauled through these hearings for relatively minor misdemeanours. The London section of BIFU saw the number of disciplinary proceedings double year-on-year during the mid-1990s. The fact that over a third of people make successful unfair dismissal claims suggests that many were tried in kangaroo courts. But, although they get some compensation, they rarely get their job back.

Holidays

Like Italy and the USA, the UK has no tradition of setting statutory minimum holiday-leave entitlements. That is changing now, however, for the UK and Italy as the European Union forces them to give their workers a break. Most Continental countries have rather more generous minimum entitlements. If UK bosses follow suit, workers in the new millennium should be aiming for six weeks off a year. The UK is also on the low side when it comes to public holidays. Spanish workers have traditionally had 14 public holidays a year, whereas their UK counterparts get just eight.

Forced holidays are, however, becoming an increasingly common feature of our insecure job market. Researchers at the Henley Centre predict that by the year 2020 'many people will be working five-hour days and have an average of one month each year without work'. You should be particularly careful about going on holiday if you feel itchy between the shoulder blades. Managers find it far less embarrassing to make staff redundant if they can do the dirty work while the people involved are away. Former Soviet Union President Mikhail Gorbachev is, perhaps, the most famous example of this phenomenon (ousted while he rested in a seaside cottage in the Crimea).

Redundancy, being sacked . . . and starting again

Most people in the workforce now should count on being made redundant at least once in their careers. On current trends, about 8 million people (one in three workers) will be fired in the next decade. Many people act like rabbits caught in the headlights. They know that disaster will hit them if they don't move, but they are too frightened to take action. If they really handle things badly, they can find that their debts build up, their homes are threatened with repossession, they can't get another job and they fight with their partners. But much of this can be avoided by planning. Most people can work out ways of making themselves more employable again. Some will find that by taking control of their own careers in this way they discover hidden talents and many new options.

Getting started

. . . .
How to write a CV

1 **Keep** it short and simple. Employers usually look for very specific qualities and abilities – including concise writing. If they can't find them in your letter, they won't invite you for interview. Accountants Coopers & Lybrand estimate that 20 per cent of job applications are too wordy.

2 **Distinguish** between applications with a CV and covering letter (usually limited to two or three paragraphs) and those where you write a letter explaining why you are suitable. These can run to a couple of pages.

3 **Don't** send the same CV to all potential employers. Experience vital to a retailer might be irrelevant to an oil company. A clever tweak can make an average application outstanding.

4 **Scrutinise** the advertisement or job description. Some employers rule you out if you omit something that you may think obvious. For example, employers who mention commitment to equal opportunities may not interview you unless you actually state your commitment.

5 **Take** the employer's perspective: highlight the ways you can help them. Saying how much you would 'enjoy the job' is a definite no-no, according to Katy Nicholson of Reed Employment: 'Employers want people who can offer something to them.'

6 **Go** for quality not quantity, especially if your first attempts fail. London University's Careers Advisory Service says, 'If you make 100 applications a week you are pretty much bound to fail. You are far better off making two applications.'

7 **Always** type a CV. Write or type your letter, or ask Personnel which they prefer.

8 **Include** hobbies. Gregarious activities – particularly team sports – go down better with large employers than pursuits that suggest you are a loner. Resist the temptation to be clever. Nicholson says, 'Don't be too loopy, esoteric or political. If you are into exorcism, don't mention it – unless it is relevant!'

· ·

How to list interests on a CV

1 **List** three to five 'interests' on your application. Never call them 'hobbies'. If you list more, your potential employers will wonder how you find time to work.

Senior managers and professionals sometimes feel embarrassed about listing activities, but it gives you a chance to show some personality and even a bit of humour. It also gives inexperienced interviewers an easy lead into the interview.

Don't list your interests as 'Reading, opera, walking and travel': you will sound dull. Say, for example, 'Member of a trekking club – hoping to walk 15 miles for Oxfam at Christmas' or 'Reading twentieth-century fiction.'

Include one sport or lively activity. This becomes more important the older you get. Also try to include one interest from the arts.

Try to include an interest that shows you can work in a team. The gentrification of football means it is less risky to list than it was. 'Team sports can be really hard for women,' says Jo Bond of Coutts Career Consultants. 'They don't tend to be in cricket teams. But they could say they work on a voluntary basis for a charity or are on a committee. It shows the same thing.'

Don't make up interests that you haven't got. Some people in sociable jobs feel they must put down 'Playing bridge at the weekends' to demonstrate their natural love of people. But decent employers understand that staff paid to be sociable often want to relax outside hours on their own.

6 **Make** sure that you can answer questions about your interests – such as 'What was the last film you saw?' If it was pornographic or violent, think of something more suitable.

7 **Never** include 'Socialising' (some recruiters will see this as evidence of a drinking problem) or 'Watching television' (97 per cent of us do, but you don't need to be quite this honest about your misspent evenings). Don't put 'Political parties', unless you are applying to join a trade union or Conservative Central Office. Also avoid religious affiliations: if you highlight them, some people will think you are a fanatic.

• •

How to prepare for a psychometric test

1 **Don't** worry that your innermost secrets will be revealed. You might be asked odd questions, but the examiners are usually looking for basic qualities, not unusual psychological disorders. Neil Scott of test administrator PSL says, 'If you are looking for a job as a bank clerk, they won't be trying to find out if you have schizophrenia. They might be looking to see how you react to stress.'

2 **Find** out in advance what kind of test you are sitting. You can improve your performance in ability tests by practice – doing mental arithmetic (for instance, adding up shopping bills in your head), or doing crosswords, puzzle books and even jigsaws. The other kind of test – personality questionnaires – is far more controversial, and it is no help to cram for them.

3 **Expect** to be tested more frequently in future. Companies are increasingly using a range of recruitment techniques, because interviews, job-simulation exercises and personality tests are unreliable on their own. Most large companies use tests in some part of their business.

4 **Don't** be put off by the length of the questionnaire. Designers of ability tests often put in too many questions deliberately to make sure that all candidates are kept busy. If you panic, it could be taken as a sign that you react badly under pressure. Questions often get harder as you go along.

5 **Expect** to *enjoy* doing a personality questionnaire. Most people like answering questions about themselves. In the simplest five-minute tests, you might have to pick out adjectives that describe you best from a list of 80. In the longer 40-minute ones, you may be asked stranger questions: 'Do you like fish? Do you read the *Observer*? What is your favourite colour?' The test administrator will, in the past, have found correlations between certain answers and, say, those of a typical accountant. There are also more obvious questionnaires that focus on particular traits – your willingness to conform, for instance. It is easy to cheat on some of these – particularly honesty tests, ironically. Neil Scott says, 'Fairly bright people can see through these questions.' No one has yet found a test that can testify to integrity or honesty.

6 **Work** out what the employer was looking for in the test before you go to any subsequent interview. If you are going for a job as a compliance officer, the test was probably looking for independence of mind and rationality, rather than other good qualities.

7 **Avoid** becoming downhearted if you are rejected. Many tests are badly designed and based on the principle that good office clerks will have the same characteristics as bureaucrats in the past. You could, for instance, be penalised for saying that your favourite colour is red and you like Thai food. Many tests reward conformity, and ability tests are often looking for a single skill – accuracy under pressure, for example – rather than overall brilliance.

••

How to deal with a recruitment agency

1 **Understand** that many agency staff will regard you as a commodity, ie in the same way that estate agents regard properties. The life of a recruitment consultant is often precarious and pressurised: their pay depends on matching you (or better candidates) with an employer, and many of them don't last more than a few months in the same position. 'They've got targets,' says former consultant Frances. 'Sometimes they will send you to interviews that they know aren't suitable.'

2 **Decide** beforehand exactly what you want from them. Someone vague and indecisive will not be regarded as dynamic and may get sent to fill the vacancies no one else wants.

3 **Look** in the appropriate advertising columns (local papers or *Accountancy Age*, for example) to see whether your qualifications or experience are in demand. HGV drivers and some pensions specialists saw dramatic rises in pay in the mid-1990s – and those that try it find they can negotiate good terms with agencies. 'Skilled temps are realising their market worth,' says Katy Nicholson of Reed Employment. 'It's worth emphasising your value to the agency.' Temps are increasingly able to demand pay rises after just a few weeks with the same agency.

4 **Prepare** for your first meeting with them as if for a job interview. If you dress smartly, they can more easily envisage you winning employers over. Ask them lots of questions ('How many vacancies do you have in this field? Which are the major employers? Will you return my calls the same day?') to find out what they can do for you. Even the best agencies employ consultants bad at their jobs. Patrick, a very successful candidate with some agencies, dealt with a number of consultants who never returned phone calls or sent him information. 'Don't deal with someone you don't like,' he says. 'It's very important that you get on well.'

5 **Sign** on with more than one agency. People who are new to the jobs market are sometimes persuaded to stick with just one. This suits the consultants, but often means you are less likely to get a job. Some of the more conscientious agencies – Manpower, for instance – need employer references going back five or ten years. You could be waiting a few weeks before they get their paperwork sorted out and before they place you. A less rigorous agency could get you something sooner.

6 Take advantage of the benefits that some agencies offer: extensive free training at Manpower and Reed, for instance; use of personal computers in many branches; assistance with writing CVs in the current fashion; paid holidays for some temporary staff; and a range of smaller perks like shopping vouchers or free accident insurance in some agencies.

How to behave in a job interview

1 Read the company's annual report, product literature, brochures and – if you want to be really impressive – its website beforehand. Try to work out the questions they will ask you and rehearse your answers. Know your CV backwards.

2 Understand that employers are increasingly looking for professionalism. 'Treat the interview as a business meeting,' says Jo Bond of Coutts Career Consultants. You can carry your papers in a folder: the annual report and your CV and application. Take extra copies of your CV (in case your interviewers do not have enough to go round) and type up a list of your referees.

Dress in the company style. You can see what people wear by waiting outside the office as people turn up for work. Women should wear suits and avoid dresses.

Smile and make eye contact with your interviewers. Be open with your body language. Talk to secretaries and other staff who may be asked their views on you. Jo Bond says, 'At the end of an interviewing day, I would always ask the secretaries whom they liked. It is important you treat that person with respect.'

Brace yourself for the old chestnut 'What are you bad/good at?' No need to mention your compulsive philandering here. Concentrate instead on 'bad' qualities that are actually good – being perhaps too committed to work, for example. You need to decide on your 'good' qualities beforehand. Everyone claims to be enthusiastic, so you should also have such marketable skills as being numerate, computer-literate and good at team-building.

Don't ramble. Try to distinguish yourself from your competitors. Malcolm Kerrell of human resource consultancy The Wildfire Corporation suggests using an image that will stick in the interviewer's mind as a label to identify you with later. For example, if you arranged a seminar for 100 people you could say that you brought along enough people to fill a double-decker bus.

Have three or four questions (no more) to ask at the end of the interview. Kerrell suggests the question, 'Where do you think this company will be in five years' time?' This, he says, gives them an opportunity to preen themselves.

8 **Consider** sending a letter to your interviewers afterwards, confirming your commitment to the role. You could pick out one or two points to emphasise in the letter, particularly if you forgot to make a crucial point in the interview. Remember that Labour leader Tony Blair was originally turned down as a candidate by his Sedgefield constituency – but managed to persuade the selection committee to reconsider.

. . . .

How to get the best from a university degree

1 **Acknowledge** that a degree, rather like A-levels 20 years ago, is a basic necessity in most sectors if you want interesting, well-paid work. One in three school-leavers now goes on to higher education, compared with one in eight in 1979. Graduates have longer careers and earn more than non-graduates. New graduates earned an average of £14,400 in 1995 – only 18 per cent less than the national average salary. If you are very smart or are in the right place at the right time (learning IT skills that turn out to be in short supply, for instance) your prospects can be unlimited without a degree, but not many people fall into this category.

2 **Expect** periods of job insecurity and unemployment. According to the *Annual Graduate Review 1996-97*, about

9 per cent of 1995 graduates were still unemployed a year later, 6 per cent were working part-time and 2 per cent were working unpaid to get experience. Later in life, you may need to take other courses or retrain completely.

3 Beware of new courses. 'There is tremendous experimentation going on,' says Nick Jagger of the Institute for Employment Studies, which publishes the *Review*. 'There is a temptation for universities to create courses that are attractive to school-leavers but not to employers.' There have been about 4,000 new degree courses a year over the past four years, raising the current level to about 40,000. When a course is in its infancy, the teaching can be patchy. Many computer science courses, for example, were initially badly thought out and badly taught.

4 Don't take vocational courses such as accountancy or law unless you are committed. Both these careers are oversubscribed, and you don't have to have a degree to enter them as a trainee. 'The degree subject is completely irrelevant,' says a spokeswoman for KPMG, which takes on 600 trainee accountants every year. (Be careful about studying philosophy, however: these graduates tend to do worse in the job market than their peers.)

5 Try hard to get a 2:1 (or Upper Second, as it's sometimes called). Some large employers (KPMG included) refuse to touch anyone with less. But don't be upset if you don't get a First. Accountant Paul Le Druillenec (2:1, Classics, Oxon.) has been involved in staff recruitment for 15 years: 'I am biased against people with Firsts. They are perfectionists. In academic life the purpose is to be absolutely right. In work, one is trying to maximise the money.' If you get a 2:2 (Lower Second) or a Third, large employers may sift you out in the first round, and you will have to find other ways to prove your worth. Many talented people do badly in undergraduate exams because they are too imaginative to conform.

6 Remind yourself that you have a ready-made network of contacts among your university contemporaries.

7 Remember the disadvantages of being a graduate. Some employers will see you as overqualified, so it can pay to play down your academic achievements. Many people feel threatened by those better qualified than themselves. Graduates on accelerated promotion schemes often need to prove their human credentials.

How to handle a criminal record

1 Think carefully about how, when and whether you will disclose your record. The National Association for the Care and Resettlement of Offenders (NACRO) says that, if requested, 'unspent' convictions should be disclosed, but it accepts that employers are often unlikely to find out the truth. NACRO believes that employers are becoming increasingly prejudiced against people with records.

2 Get some training and education. NACRO believes that an increasing number of training organisations are developing a positive attitude to ex-offenders. Patrick

FitzGibbon (not his real name), who spent three years in jail for grievous bodily harm before going to university and becoming a social worker, says, 'Access to choice and information reduces the possibility of reoffending. The majority of criminals have very limited experience.'

3 Network. People who know you are more likely than strangers to give you the benefit of the doubt.

4 Consider how you might become self-employed. Some people with a record will never persuade an employer to take them on. The problem in setting up your own business is lack of capital, so many people start off small – as couriers, window cleaners, painters, etc.

5 Get the books and leaflets: NACRO has some free guides, including *Declaring Convictions*, (tel. 0171-582 6500 for a copy); the Apex Trust sells a booklet, *Straight for Work* (£2.90, tel. 0171-638 5931). Some probation and careers offices have copies of *I Can't Do That, Can I?*, published by the Avon Education, Training and Careers Guidance Service, but now out of print. *Just for the Record* is available free from Job Centres.

6 Talk to your family. FitzGibbon says, 'Your family deep down disapproves of what you have done but they will support you, and want you to change and do something with your life. That is the nature of families.' According to Home Office statistics, 34 per cent of men and 8 per cent of women have criminal convictions by the age of 40.

How to behave on your first day

Arrive early and tend towards the subfusc rather than outlandish in your dress. 'When you went for the interview you probably dressed like something out of a Harrods window,' says Malcolm Kerrell of human resource consultancy The Wildfire Corporation. 'They won't expect you to look the same now, but don't look like a reject from Murphy's builders either. Take out the nose ring.'

'Listen, smile and keep your mouth shut,' says Tess Lever, a former civil servant and expert in office politics. 'In an organisation that is split into armed camps, people will try to recruit you to their side. Don't get drawn in.'

Start your intelligence-gathering campaign, remembering that knowledge is power. Take advantage of your newcomer status to ask questions, both about the practicalities of how things are done and about the firm's culture.

Don't miss the opportunity to have lunch or drinks after work with your new colleagues. The sooner you get to know them, the more quickly you will feel at home.

Get to know the people who really matter: the secretaries, receptionists, people in charge of accommodation and messengers. Your boss's secretary is perhaps the most important person from your point of view.

6 **Remember** that most people feel nervous in a new job. Don't overcompensate by bragging about how good your last company was.

7 **Understand** that you do not have to do your job in the same way your predecessor did – but you have to be tactful if you want to make changes. Talk to people in different parts of the organisation, not just your peers – they are accustomed to the *status quo*.

· ·

How to make the best out of a boring job

1 **Grin** and bear it if your job is a means to an end. If you are a bored trainee accountant or lawyer, for example, it is possible to stifle your imagination until you qualify.

2 **Ask** yourself why you are underachieving. If you are bored, it means you are capable of doing more. Your job may be at risk in the long term: technology is doing away with many tedious jobs. Your personality may also be at risk. Nadia Sharples, a former manager in a utilities company, met many bored people when she worked in management: 'Frustrated, bored people are terrible. Boredom breaks hearts and spirits. They become barrack-room lawyers and office politicians, but not in a positive way. They want to subvert the system.'

3 **Get** any training you can. If you are a secretary or clerk, you might be able to get training in IT or health and safety – skills that you can use as a selling-point later.

4 **Volunteer.** Contribute articles to your company newsletter, become active in the union, agree to do the jobs that your superiors have difficulty farming out.

5 **Understand** that boredom is often the result of fear. It is easier to say that you are bored than admit you are frightened about your ability to cope with new demands.

6 **Recognise** the danger signs. If you are often sick for no reason, if you can't get out of bed in the morning, if you always leave work on time, something is wrong.

7 **Don't** hold out for your pension. In the past many people sacrificed a lifetime's boredom for a secure income in retirement. Now that even the Inland Revenue and the Department of Social Security are making redundancies, no one's job is safe.

How to get a summer job

1 **Aim** high. Even though there is strong competition for the jobs on Caribbean and Mediterranean cruise ships, *someone* has to get them. If you fail, you can still get something interesting if you research the market. In Reading, for example, the Jobcentre, places staff for the Ascot and Windsor races.

2 **Apply** early. Many of the best jobs are sorted out in spring. Visit Jobcentres and temporary agencies; apply directly to employers. But the best starting point is probably a guide such as *Summer Jobs Britain* or *Summer Jobs Abroad* (published by Vacation Work and available in bookshops or on 01865 241 978).

3 **Don't** expect an easy summer. *Summer Jobs* editor David Woodworth ruined a pair of jeans on a day's raspberry-picking stint in Cheshire several years ago: 'You're not going to earn a fortune fruit-picking, and you are going to get cold and wet. But, on the other hand, a lot of camaraderie can build up.'

4 **Decide** whether you want an interesting, a well paid or an enjoyable job: you probably can't have them all. Holiday camps are heavily staffed by students working as anything from lifeguard or cartoon character to cleaner or ride attendant. But the pay can be as little as £50 a week plus board and lodging. Factory work will be less sociable and may involve shift work and early starts, but the money is often better than in leisure and tourism.

5 **Accept** that many employers prefer someone who can work the full season. An obvious exception is fruit-picking, where you will have to lead a nomadic existence if you are looking for employment throughout the summer and early autumn.

6 **Build** up experience, particularly if you want to work abroad. French balloon companies are showing a liking for English staff – but language skills and a track record will make you seem a more reliable proposition. Many employers (the Post Office, for instance) give first refusal to people who have worked there before.

7 **Avoid** areas of high unemployment. Getting a job in Northern Ireland will be more difficult than in London. Spain, with an unemployment rate of more than 20 per cent, offers far fewer opportunities than France.

8 **Understand** that the experience you gain could prove invaluable for the rest of your life. If you can't get paid employment, some voluntary work will give you contacts and connections. Even if you loathe your job, it will show you what to avoid.

Pay and conditions

How to read an employment contract

1 **Be** wary of an unlimited hours clause. Many employers say that you must work the hours necessary to do the job, so you could find yourself working night and day, in theory. Many employees end up doing large amounts of unpaid overtime. Similarly, be wary of a clause that says you can be asked to change your place of work to another part of the country.

2 **See** whether there is a variation clause. This is intended to give your employer considerable latitude if they want to change the terms and conditions of employment.

3 **Look** out for your redundancy terms. These are often contained in another document, such as a union agreement or a paper by the personnel department.

4 **Collect** the other documents that make up your contract. The item that Personnel gives you (usually called something like the 'Statement of principal terms of employment') is only a part. You will also be bound by such things as health and safety guidelines, statements from Personnel, agreements between your employer and the union, and letters from your employer.

5 Scrutinise your job description. Broad phrasing could mean that you can be asked to make dramatic job changes. If your employer wants to make life difficult for you, a loose job description will make it easier for him to ask you to start cleaning out the lavatories.

6 Check basic details: pay, notice periods on both sides, holiday entitlement, and rights to be reimbursed for expenses. Personnel departments can make mistakes.

7 Read the fine print. For instance, some companies will slip in a clause preventing you from accruing holiday entitlements when you are ill. Many employers have restrictive-trade clauses that prevent you from setting up business in competition with them for long periods after you leave. Agreeing to this could leave you without a livelihood later on.

How to negotiate a pay rise

1 Focus your attentions on the right person. Many personnel departments exist to keep pay levels down: if you are good at your job, your boss may be more sympathetic.

2 **Prepare** your case. Highlight your achievements – particularly those that make a financial difference to your employer. If the company earns income that is clearly attributable to you, you are in a strong position. Appreciative letters from clients demonstrate this.

3 **Collect** information about what other people in your industry earn. Stifle, flaunt or ignore it as appropriate. Get the background information too – inflation rates, in particular.

4 **Consider** redefining your job. Technology and increasing competition give scope for change, expanding responsibilities and (therefore) more pay.

5 **Get** your timing right – in terms of your employer's finances, annual budget and your boss's moods. The anniversary of your arrival is always a useful date.

6 **Don't** threaten to leave unless you can afford to carry out the threat. Although your threat may achieve results in the short term, it will probably be long remembered as a symptom of your underlying disloyalty. But threats do produce results. Nick Robbins of legal recruitment consultancy Garfield Robbins says, 'There's a move towards counter-offers when people say they are going to leave. And there's also an increase in counter-counter-offers. There is a shortage of top people.' One gazumping saw a City solicitor increase his annual salary by £100,000 without leaving his firm.

7 **Don't** be too cocky in describing your abilities. If you are the best in your field, you might logically want to earn all your salary in the form of performance-related pay.

. . . .

How to deal with the threat of a pay cut

1 **Work** out the motives. Companies can often find legal ways of cutting pay if they are struggling for survival. But some will plead poverty even while increasing directors' earnings.

2 **Brace** yourself for a bout of brinkmanship. Cornwall Care, which faced £500,000 costs after losing a crucial industrial tribunal ruling in April 1997, said it could fold; it claimed that 250 careworkers who won their case against pay cuts may now lose their jobs.

3 **Put** your objections in writing to the company immediately if it unilaterally decides to reduce pay. You can then bring an industrial tribunal claim for an unlawful deduction from pay under the Employment Rights Act 1996, backdated to the date of your letter. You do not have to leave the company to make your claim.

4 **Be** sceptical if your employer offers new contracts. This is sometimes a way of reducing pay or other benefits, such as health insurance or subsidised meals. Employers sometimes use subtle ways of introducing cuts. Many employees agree to new terms. Dissenters are often dismissed, but can claim unfair dismissal, unless they have been with the company less than two years.

5 **Understand** that some employers are ignorant of the law. Your rights to your current pay level should still be preserved if your department is transferred to another contractor. Many people who once worked for local authorities lost money when this provision was ignored. Employers who do not follow statutory consultation procedures when at least 20 staff are given new terms may have to pay up to four weeks' salary in damages to each individual.

6 **Aim** to show a united front. 'If the employees stay solid, then the employer could have no staff and a very expensive unfair dismissal claim,' says James Davies of solicitors Lewis Silkin. 'If there are 20 or 30 employees affected, the employer might accept that one or two will bring claims.'

7 **Understand** that many people quickly decide that a badly paid job is better than no job. There is usually room for negotiation with good employers who will want your co-operation to prevent a fall in morale. Acton Law Shop has seen people accept reduced hours for reduced pay. The cut might also be made temporary, and made good retrospectively if business turns up.

How to get the best out of working part-time

1 **Understand** that your legal position has improved dramatically in the last few years and will get better still. No longer a Cinderella, you should gradually be moving up market. For example, both part- and full-timers are to qualify for unfair dismissal rights after one year of service rather than two. In the past, millions of part-timers had no such rights at all. In April 1998 Employment Minister Ian McCartney signed up the UK to the EU directive on part-time workers, saying, 'We are committed to part-time workers having at least the same rights as full-time workers.' Thank your lucky stars that it was radical reformer Margaret Beckett who ran the Department of Trade and Industry at this crucial time rather than one of her more conservative colleagues.

2 **Encourage** your employer to give you the same benefits package as full-timers. By April 2000, when the EU part-time work directive is implemented here, most employers should have harmonised their packages. But, as with most employment laws, some companies may be too shifty or too confused to comply. 'They run the risk of expensive claims against them,' says employment specialist Chris Booth of law firm Pinsent Curtis. You may want to wave a copy of the directive (available through the European Commission office in London, or the Department of Trade and Industry) at your personnel department.

3 **Watch** out for the common traps: overtime, pensions and company cars. 'Full-time workers typically get one-and-a-half times pay for overtime,' says Richard Lynch of banking union BIFU. 'But part-timers often get conned by being paid at the normal rate.' Many part-time workers find they get a tiny company pension – because they are members of an 'integrated' scheme, to which their employer makes no contribution on their first £3,400 of earnings. Company cars are a particular problem: it is not easy to give someone two-fifths of a vehicle. 'But it may be possible to equate the benefits in monetary terms,' says Booth.

4 **Look** for help from your union or the Equal Opportunities Commission (EOC) (tel. 0161-833 9244) if you think you are being unfairly treated. Because about four out of five part-time workers are female, the EOC plays a large role in defending women's rights. Many successful cases have been taken against employers on grounds of indirect sex discrimination – a major no-no in the politically correct world of the EU.

5 **Keep** in particularly close contact with your boss, warns Sylvia Kalisch, a former part-time worker who now manages others. 'If you aren't there every day, you don't always get the full picture – and might not get all the chances you would otherwise have.' Because bosses tend to allocate projects as they come up, you could benefit from making clear your particular interests in advance.

How to plan your pension

1 Find out whether your scheme provides life cover (most do) and a spouse's or dependant's pension. Many people buy unnecessary life assurance because they do not read the information that their own pensions department puts out. If you are co-habiting or have a dependant who is not your spouse, you may be able to suggest them as your intended beneficiary if you die – but you must inform the pension scheme trustees.

2 Get the benefit of your employer's contributions. The combination of tax relief and employer contributions may mean that your payments into the pension are, in effect, trebled or quadrupled. You are usually best advised to join the pension scheme as soon as you can and to pay as much as you can into it.

3 Read both the general scheme literature and the statements that set out your personal position to find out whether you will be underfunded, as many people are, in retirement. Peter Murray of the National Association of Pension Funds says, 'Your retirement will last a long time, and you will need a lot of money to provide for it.'

4 Ask your pensions department to explain anything you do not understand. The people there tend to be evangelists who will spend time talking to you. Personnel departments do not always know much about pensions. In a 'money purchase' scheme, for example, you are building up an investment with which you will later buy a pension annuity – a plan that pays you a fixed income each year. In a 'final salary' scheme, your employer contracts to pay you a pension equal to a proportion of your salary at retirement. Money purchase schemes are becoming more popular because the employee, not the employer, shoulders the investment risk.

5 **Consider** carefully before transferring your accumulated pension fund if you change employers. If you are in a good, secure scheme where, for example, benefits are index-linked and the trustees have a history of giving discretionary improvements, you would need a lot of inducements to transfer. Timing – in relation to long-term gilts rates – is critical if you are transferring from a final-salary scheme. Bad timing can leave you 20 to 30 per cent worse off.

6 **Pay** additional voluntary contributions (AVCs) if you can. Most people making AVCs are in their fifties, but your funds have much longer to grow if you start before then.

7 **Keep** an eye on your money. If you are in a final-salary scheme you should join – or, if necessary, set up – a pensioners' committee. When you retire, argue for benefits increases and monitor investments policy. If you are in a money purchase scheme, you can increase your retirement income substantially by scouring the market for good annuity rates. Some pension schemes recommend annuities that are not particularly good value. Only three out of ten pensioners have a large enough income to have to pay tax.

How to safeguard your company pension

1 Be suspicious if you don't hear from your pension trustees at least once a year. Pensioners and people paying contributions should get an annual report and other notifications of changes taking place. Deferred members – people who have changed companies but left their pension funds behind – get less documentation, but still need to keep in contact.

2 Read, even briefly, everything you get – particularly accounts. Keep old reports and make comparisons. Andrew Powell of solicitors Hammond Suddards says, 'If the fund was £142 million last year and is now £98 million, you would want to know why.'

3 Scrutinise the 'asset allocation'. Two-thirds of investments will typically be in listed equities and the remaining third in fixed-interest products, property and cash. Large, risky investments – unquoted shares, small companies, property or the employer's other businesses, for example – should raise your suspicions, says actuary William Mercer.

4 Don't assume perfection. Small companies are statistically most at risk – but bigger ones get into trouble too. Few personnel departments understand pensions: expect some errors if they, rather than pensions specialists, run the scheme. Using your common sense could avoid a Robert Maxwell-style milking of assets. Powell says,

'People in the Maxwell organisation thought that some-one very important would run things properly. That is a big mistake.' A spokesman for the Occupational Pensions Regulatory Authority (OPRA), says, 'The workforce might be mistakenly reassured if they know there are cashflow problems but see a charismatic entrepreneur who doesn't seem to be affected by the bad times.'

5 **Voice** suspicions quickly to the scheme trustees. The Pension Schemes Registry (tel. 0191-225 6393) can trace schemes and trustees. If you think the fault lies with the trustees, you could contact the scheme actuaries or audi-tors, anonymously if you wish. They have a duty to contact OPRA if they are worried. OPRA runs a hotline (tel. 01273 627600) and offers free copies of its booklet, *Spotlight on OPRA* and factsheet, *A Problem with your Company Pension? A guide to who can help you*.

6 **Blow** the whistle immediately if your contributions are being diverted or paid in late. These are criminal offences and a sign that your company is probably on the verge of collapse. If your money goes into company accounts rather than the pension scheme, a receiver may try to use it to pay the bills.

Becoming successful

How to be assertive

1 **Understand** the basic thinking behind the growth in assertiveness training. Assertiveness is seen as the healthy alternative to three unhealthy ways of relating to other people: aggression, passivity and manipulation. Women more often err by being passive, giving feeble handshakes, suppressing their resentments and starting sentences with 'This is probably a stupid point but . . .'. Most people are straightforward in their dealings with others when they are relaxed, but they often fall back into bad habits learnt in childhood when they are brought into conflict. People who flounce out of meetings may achieve their short-term aim, but they lose the respect of colleagues in the longer term.

2 **Avoid** sitting with your feet on your desk and your hands behind your head as you talk to colleagues or subordinates. Unless they also have the right to sit in this posture in front of you, then it may be seen as subtly aggressive (usually male) behaviour. Debra Allcock, assertiveness specialist at the Industrial Society, says, 'If you use arrogant body language, you stop the other person from being natural with you. You set them up in a subordinate position. Assertiveness is about making yourself equal to other people.'

3 Start to think about what you want to achieve at work, both in the long term and as regards individual projects and meetings. 'It is difficult to be assertive until you are clear about your own visions and values,' says Jo Bond of Coutts Career Consultants. Assertiveness specialists suggest a few basic steps at meetings, confrontations or other discussions: decide what you want, state it openly, listen carefully and imaginatively to the other person, and then hold your negotiations and reach a practical compromise.

4 Resist the temptation to feel embarrassed at speaking your mind. Management structures have changed dramatically in the last few years. People are increasingly being encouraged to speak up and negotiate as a way of representing their own department or cost centre.

5 Back up your assertive outlook by developing a more confident physical appearance. If you are dressed inappropriately or walk with a shuffle, you are less likely to be treated equally. Staff trainers encourage people to look others in the eye; smile when on the telephone ('It comes through in the voice,' says Bond); recognise the presence of others by saying hello and good-bye and shaking hands; and pay more attention generally to the rights and obligations of themselves and others.

6 **Avoid** stirring up negative emotions. Instead of shouting 'Why are you late, you lazy devil?' at your colleague, Allcock suggests that you say, 'When you are late, I have to answer your telephone.' Avoid asking the person why he or she is late: it is in the past and does not really matter. Say what you want to happen in the future – for example, 'Will you ring me if you know you are going to be late?'

7 **Don't** let yourself be blown off course by the other person's reaction. Think through your discussion beforehand if you expect it to be difficult; decide, for instance, how far you are prepared to compromise. But if your colleague gets angry, don't respond in kind. On rare occasions you will deliberately decide to be passive, manipulative or aggressive, if you are dealing with a disturbed character or a difficult child, or are in a dangerous situation that has to be resolved quickly.

How to manage your time

1 **Appreciate** the benefits of being efficient: no more key-hunts each time you leave home; grovelling sessions when you arrive late and unbriefed for meetings; or working days that run to 12 hours. Ronald Reagan and Winston Churchill both delegated and did the business in a few hours a day, leaving plenty of time for other, more enjoyable pursuits.

2 **Stop** blaming colleagues or your workload if you do long hours. 'A lot of people waste time moaning about how busy they are,' says Judi James of the Industrial Society. She strongly recommends training: 'Time management is one of the most effective courses you can go on. It changes people's whole working lives.' The most efficient people often leave work at 5 pm. The late-stayers are often worried about their jobs or are poor at making decisions. In *Managing Workplace Stress* psychologists Susan Cartwright and Cary Cooper write: 'Procrastination often stems from boredom, a lack of confidence, or reluctance to seek clarification.' It is frequently better to take a decision (even if it is the wrong one) than to delay.

3 **Keep** a log of your time for a few days, suggests James. 'People can quite cheerfully waste up to two hours a day – perhaps listening to others moaning, trying unsuccessfully to get people on the phone, looking for lost bits of paper.' Set aside some time – an hour every day or two – to think about your longer-term aims and how you are achieving them. How are you going to fulfil your company's sales targets for this year?

4 **Start** making lists – a habit of most efficient people. You might have five main aims for the year (increase the membership of the golf club you run, perhaps). These then translate into medium-term aims (compare advertising rates in the local papers) and things to do tomorrow (get Dolly's opinion on the copy for the ad you have booked).

5 **Delegate**. An inefficient boss will check all the letters that his or her juniors send out – with the usual result that no one gets a reply within five months. The better you are, the more demands there can be on your time. Occupational psychologist Michael Carroll of consultancy Right Cavendish says, 'Good managers are good listeners, so everyone wants to speak to them. So the manager has to say "Am I the person you want to speak to? You might be better speaking to X first, and then coming back to me."'

6 Concentrate fully on each job you do. Aim to get it right first time and to get into the habit of finishing every task you start. Capitalise on your enthusiasm when you are feeling in good spirits, and avoid flogging yourself when you feel tired and bored.

7 Don't keep other people waiting. People who ramble at meetings are wasting the time of 12 people, not just their own. Allow some selective queue-jumping: if a customer asks for the pepper, a waitress won't keep him waiting until she has first dealt with the seven requests she got from other diners.

How to get the credit for your successes

1 Don't snipe at colleagues and don't steal credit that is due to them. Some people are always generous in giving the credit, but most operate on the principle of 'What goes around comes around.'

Create a climate in which credit is shared, and thank your colleagues: praise always sounds better coming from someone else. See how political leaders at international summits often eulogise each other. This public back-slapping helps all of them by improving their reputations and suggesting an atmosphere of well-being and *bonhomie*.

Take a long-term view. People will not give you the credit if they do not understand your job. Discuss a new job or role with your bosses: identify your reporting structures and measurements of success. People who do this are less likely to end up as fall-guys if things go wrong.

Write memos outlining your role and noting any decisions or actions taken, particularly if you believe that someone else will be trying to take your Brownie points.

Try to reduce any craving you have for recognition. Psychotherapist Frances Wilks, director of personal development courses at City University, believes genuine praise is more likely to go to those who do not demand it: 'Decide if you are going to give yourself the credit. You are the most important judge of that. If you do, it will ripple outwards.'

Understand that many of the best performers are never recognised. Anti-slavery campaigner William Wilberforce was, in some ways, a front man for activities masterminded by others. Former teacher Holly Dickens maintains that Thomas Gray's *Elegy* applies as much to the workplace as to public life: 'You have to decide whether you want your ideas carried out or whether you want the credit. If you want the ideas carried out, you give other people the credit.'

∙∙

How to get more training

1 **Understand** the disadvantages first. While you are getting educated, others are making money. Well-paid finance directors are less likely to have MBAs or advanced university degrees than their poorer colleagues, according to a 1997 survey by NBS Selection. Only 12 per cent of finance directors earning about £70,000 have MBAs, compared with 22 per cent of those earning £45,000. Richard Branson is typical of many entrepreneurs in not having needed extensive formal education.

2 **Accept** that training will change your aspirations. Many people who take MBAs become disillusioned and isolated and leave their old jobs.

3 **Realise**, however, that learning through work is becoming increasingly important. The Labour government elected in 1997 with its priorities of 'education, education, education' has stated its intention to encourage 'lifelong learning' to make people more self-sufficient in the workplace. The rapid development of technology alone means that people become out of date, and less employable, unless they keep in touch.

4 **Adapt** to the training environment of your employer. Only 11 per cent of companies can be described as 'learning organisations', according to the Industrial Society. This means you will have to take the initiative to get training in most businesses. You could find there is a budget marked 'Training' going to waste.

5 **Choose** employers that emphasise training. You can, for example, work in a bar, which adds little to your CV, or get formal training from such a chain as All Bar One, which coaches its staff in a range of subjects from wines and spirits to customer service.

6 **Take** as much training as you can if your job is routine. Tesco, for instance, trains all its staff – but has shifted towards shorter, less standardised courses. Ask in your appraisals for training. Bosses will be more likely to send you on courses that help you do your job, but if you word requests carefully ('I can cover for Henry if I learn till procedures'), you can expand your empire.

7 **Understand** the need to make sacrifices. You can probably get colleagues to train you in Word for Windows or e-mail, but you may have to arrange this in your spare time. Alternatively, your employer might agree to give you time off for a course – but perhaps won't pay your tuition fees. Individuals will increasingly start paying to go on courses themselves; this is already starting to happen in the field of personal development, where growing numbers of people (mainly women) are being coached in assertiveness and other 'soft skills'. Some of the more advanced trade unions (BIFU, the banking union, for instance) already provide free training.

8 **Don't** be overambitious. Imperial College Management School, provider of the Civil Service MBA, runs a part-time course with seminars on alternate Fridays over two years. 'People do not concentrate at this level in the evenings,' says course director Joe Tidd. The fall-out rate for distance learning is also high, because students get no peer support and can take several years to complete a given course.

······································

How to keep up with office gossip

1 **Fraternise** with the smokers. Barred from smoking at their desks, they get together in corridors for a smoke . . . and a chat. Smoking brings together people of different ranks and departments who would never normally meet.

2 **Cultivate** secretaries, post-room staff, receptionists and messengers. They know who is coming and going – potential recruits, policemen, receivers, for example. They also know the habits of the senior staff.

3 **Meet** the temporary staff, especially if they work in departments other than your own. Temps can know more about the business as a whole than people who work full-time.

4 Don't get a reputation for being the office gossip yourself. Your bosses won't trust you and your colleagues will ridicule you. But do trade bits of gossip. Good gossip-flows are like trade links: they need to work in both directions.

5 Recognise the importance of gossip. You may get indications about future redundancies or new bosses. By being ahead of the rest you may be able, for example, to get a more comfortable chair or work with more pleasant colleagues.

6 Avoid asking direct questions of senior personnel or accounts staff (unless they have had too much to drink). They are trained to be on their guard for people like you.

7 Keep in contact with any trade union representative – usually a source of facts and figures as well as gossip.

8 Read notice boards, trade magazines and newspapers. Some of the best-kept secrets are published but not read by the people who would most benefit from knowing them. Rumours were circulating about trader Nick Leeson a full year before the collapse of Barings.

How to get promotion

1 Work out whether the notorious 'glass ceiling' exists in your company. Managers (especially if they own the business) tend to promote 'people like us' if they can get away with it. The first female pioneers in the police force, such as Alison Halford, were bound to get a hard time. Their equivalents in the City are still frequently in the 'superwoman' mould – having babies at the weekend and back at the desk on Monday (if they have children at all). Should this sort of struggle not be your cup of tea, you'd be better off looking for somewhere more in tune with your personality.

Recognise that your first promotions will usually come from people a generation older than you. If your employers run a conservative company, they may hold your pony-tail or casual dress against you.

Show willing by getting some qualifications under your belt. Some insurance companies have threatened to bar promotion to people who have not passed the industry exams. Certain fields (estate agents and financial services, for instance) are desperate to present themselves as professionals to the world. Their employees will come under pressure to get letters after their name – even though the exams aren't always that demanding.

Get yourself the title 'deputy'. You never know what could befall your boss – and then you would be almost automatically 'acting head'. No one ever tipped Lyndon B. Johnson to become US president – until J. F. Kennedy went to Dallas. Many promotions take place by accident: you happen to be the only one with experience of running a team, people like you, and you have a driving licence.

5 **Decide** exactly what job you want, and decide how, over a year perhaps, you will get there. The best plans are usually long term. If you need to demonstrate leadership, for instance, you can find an excuse to make a short speech – a word of thanks to the bosses at the Christmas party or an address in your new voluntary position of pension scheme trustee.

6 **Ask** your boss or someone sympathetic what you have to do to get promotion. Not only will you gain useful information, but you might also get a backer of your cause.

7 **Don't** lose heart if you don't get there. Traditional selection procedures reflect the assumptions of the people designing them – and may be unable to distinguish genuine talent from the mere semblance of it. The Foreign Office used selection procedures based on World War Two officer recruitment techniques until the 1980s. You might never advance in this kind of framework, but you might flourish elsewhere.

How to get a seat on the board

1 **Look** at current board members and behave and dress as they do. If they all wear broad pinstripes and have hearty laughs, you can gradually develop that way. Many boards are terrified of admitting people who will make their lives uncomfortable. Wait until you become a director before revealing your non-conformist tendencies.

2 **Work** out how board appointments are made. Most companies choose from among department heads, but some look for broader skills. The finance director will nearly always be on the board, but personnel or IT heads may have to demonstrate a good case.

3 **Understand** that board members in well-run companies have a far more elevated role than department heads. Angela Vint of consultancy the Success Group says, 'The role of the director is to create a vision, decide strategy and set an example to the staff. Managers are there to organise resources.' The days of regularly propping up the bar are over: you need *gravitas*.

4 **Make** your ambition known to the board. If you wait for your qualities to be recognised, you could be waiting a long time. Many people get close to one particular board member who then acts as their mentor and advocate. If you already work for the company, you will probably come cheaper than people recruited from outside. But even small companies will usually top up your salary by at least £3,000 when you join the board, says Vint. Nearly all directors earn at least £35,000; many earn far more.

5 **Recognise** that you can be in considerable demand as a non-executive director. 'The people who are really needed are becoming more cautious about appointments,' says Charlotte Boyce of recruitment service ProNed. A greater emphasis on the responsibilities of non-executives means that the job should rarely be regarded as the sinecure it often was. The workload is normally between

20 and 40 days a year and pay, depending on the hours and the size of the company, usually starts at £15,000.

How to give a pep talk

1 **Don't** overdo the sentiment. You are likely to find that workers are less overtly emotional about their jobs than the bosses. A senior banking executive once started a pep talk by standing mute for 60 seconds and then declaring: 'I love this company.' His audience, who all earned far less than him, were not so infatuated – and felt embarrassed.

2 **Mix** the rousing parts of your talk with facts and arguments. Few people have the oratorical skills of a Martin Luther King; most will have to produce hard evidence to back up their assertions. The best talks tend to use a wide range of devices – anecdotes, analogies, jokes and examples.

3 **Structure** your presentation around two or three messages. As well as trying to encourage your colleagues, you may need to point them in a new direction. The messages should be easy to grasp: 'We aren't afraid of the competition. . . can do things to beat them. . . and have the skilled workforce to deliver. . .'. Save the more complicated themes for smaller groups. Sermons from the pulpit often fall on deaf ears, particularly if they are a collection of unrelated homilies and views rather than a sustained argument.

4 **Abide** by the usual rules of rhetoric, unless you are very gifted. Rousing starts, crescendo finales and three-part examples are all useful techniques. Even the most experienced people can make mistakes: at the 1997 Conservative Party conference, chairman Cecil Parkinson paid an unexpected compliment to Labour leader Tony Blair and paused for his audience to react; after some moments of silence, he prompted them with 'You're supposed to clap.' Pitch your presentations as if you are talking to 'an intelligent 15-year-old', is the advice contained in the Nobo Presentation Guide: 'Avoid two classic traps: being seen as patronising; and over-estimating [your audience's] knowledge by using technical terms and jargon.'

5 **Consider** focusing some of your praise on one or two notable performers. Many managers choose an employee who will not be seen as a threat to others: the secretary who organised the annual dinner or the tea lady 'who always cheers us up with her wonderful smile'. But, unless you choose someone deserving, you could be seen as capricious and prone to favouritism.

6 **Be** careful about giving your staff a dressing-down in the hope that this will encourage them to work harder. Harsh words are better said in private to the transgressors. Collective rebukes often stay in the memory and can be especially resented by the more diligent. A common defence mechanism among the admonished is to turn the chastiser into a figure of fun.

Overcoming difficulties

How to deal with a bully

1 **Diagnose** your problem. Bullying, a power game intended to make the victim lose self-respect and confidence, is a subtle art. Although the stereotypical bully is a male middle manager, women and junior staff can also be bullies. Bullying is sometimes obvious (the man who shouts at his colleague when the MD is around), but it is often devious (the secretary who sets up the boss by, for example, leaving confidential papers lying around and forgetting to pass on important information).

2 **Keep** a diary. Elaine Bennett – a former victim of bullying and now a trainer for the Industrial Society – suggests a record of 'what was said, the circumstances, who witnessed it, and how long it went on'.

3 **Try** to get the bully to stop. If you cannot talk to them, perhaps a colleague could intervene.

4 **Talk** to someone: your boss, the personnel department or your trade union representative. Large companies, such as the Midland Bank and Littlewoods, are introducing anti-bullying policies.

5 Consider making a claim under the relevant race and sex discrimination laws (the Race Relations Act 1976 and the Sex Discrimination Act 1975). You can make a claim even if you have worked in the business for less than one year – the threshold due to be introduced in 1999 for many employment rights.

6 Be wary of quitting and lodging a constructive dismissal claim – the other main legal remedy if the bullying is neither racist nor sexist. 'It is notoriously difficult to prove in these cases,' says Anna Barlow of the Acton Law Shop in West London. In some cases, the best advice is to look for another job.

7 See your doctor if it is getting you down. 'People don't tell the doctor enough for the doctor to realise that stress could be the cause of [their] problems,' says Elaine Bennett. The Industrial Society estimates that on average each UK employee is off work for three days a year because of stress and mental illness.

How to react if you have an accident

1 Report the accident to your superiors and log it with Personnel. If there has been physical injury, take photographs of any visible marks.

'Visit your doctor even if you don't think you are badly hurt,' says employment solicitor James Davies of Lewis Silkin. 'People sometimes find that down the line they start to have headaches or some other symptom.' To win compensation you will need to prove that you suffered as a direct result of the accident.

Consider whether you have a financial claim. If you spilt tea over yourself because you are clumsy, it is difficult to blame your company. But if you were making tea for your boss in a badly lit kitchen with a slippery floor, your case would be substantially strengthened.

Remember that employees are generally in a strong bargaining position on health and safety issues. Your employers have a duty to provide a safe working environment and are required by law to insure for health and safety claims. Companies can be prosecuted in the criminal courts. The laws are often improved. Since 1996 employers have also had to consult with employees (or their representatives), monitor health and safety issues regularly and have risk assessments.

Don't worry about reporting an accident or raising any concerns. 'Your employer cannot sack or discipline you for complaining about health and safety,' says Davies.

Consult a solicitor or, better still, your union if you think you may have a claim. Legal proceedings may have to be initiated, but cases are usually settled before going to court. Fergus Whitty, legal director of the Transport and

General Workers' Union, says the union is successful in 75 per cent of the cases it takes on.

●●

How to recover from a *faux pas*

1 **Plan** in advance, because a *faux pas* can happen to anyone. Former civil servant Lucia O'Loughlin has contingency plans for the day when her knickers fall down at a conference: 'I will put them in my handbag, laugh and say something like "I've been waiting for this moment all my life," or "It could happen to a Reverend Mother".'

2 **Know** your weaknesses. Some people specialise in forgetting names, others in forgetting faces, and others say silly things when they get nervous. If you are bad with names, for example, have some stock get-outs such as: 'I'm sorry, I can't remember my own name some days.'

3 **Apologise** immediately. You are likely to snuff out any irritation if you respond straight away, but if you leave it five minutes your apologies will seem late and clumsy.

4 **Remember** that you can score large numbers of Brownie points if you make a joke of the issue rather than looking embarrassed. 'People love to see other people making a fool of themselves. They are glad they didn't do it,' says O'Loughlin. People will remember your reaction ('Didn't Bloggins come out of that one well?') just as much as the incident itself. Very often, however, you can get away with saying nothing. If you look confident, people often don't register your errors.

5 **Find** a confessor if you have not been able to laugh at the time and want to make a public correction of your mistake. If your fly was undone when you made a presentation to colleagues, you can be sure they will be talking about it afterwards. If you talk about it to one or two colleagues yourself, word will probably get round that you, too, see the funny side.

6 **Let** others know you do not mind being on the receiving end. They will be grateful for your jollity.

7 **Remember** that you can salvage many situations by appearing confident. Alison Sutherland of public relations consultancy AVS Publicity recommends a swift, direct approach if one person in a group is making the others cringe: 'Change the subject.' If the rest of the audience is with you, you can sometimes stop an embarrassing talk by premature and prolonged applause.

•••

How to deal with a drink problem

1 **Recognise** that you could lose your job. Many employers will never raise the subject but none the less find excuses to get rid of drinkers. The search for greater productivity means that people who regularly suffer from hangovers are likely to be targeted.

2 **Find** out whether your employer is one of the 50 per cent who have 'alcohol policies'. These outline your rights and duties, along with the appropriate procedures.

3 **Consider** talking to your personnel department – but only if the company has an alcohol policy and appears sympathetic. An intermediary could be useful. Alcohol Concern, which advises companies, says many employers can be trusted and will give you time off for counselling. A spokesman says, 'The biggest problem is the vast majority of people who drink a little bit too much or who drink inappropriately on occasions. Most people can deal with these problems with a little bit of education.' If you choose this route, you will be expected to sort out your problem (but not necessarily to stop drinking) in a few months.

4 **Don't** drink at lunchtime in your office or in the staff canteen.

5 **Diagnose** your problem. The government has estimated that more than 8.5 million people drink over 'sensible limits' and three million are defined as 'problem' drinkers. Personnel departments are starting to look for subtle signs.

6 **Understand** that if your employer starts disciplinary proceedings, it may take over six months to get rid of you. Janet Gaymer of solicitors Simmons and Simmons says, 'Dealing with someone with a deep-rooted problem can be difficult because it is often not easy to have a rational conversation.'

7 **All** is not lost if you turn up drunk at work just the once. Mitigating circumstances often outweigh the charges of misconduct that might be brought. Twice as many women drinkers as men contacted the government-funded Drinkline (tel. 0345 320202). The average employee was off work for about five hours in 1997 because of excessive drinking.

How to cope if you are bad at your job

1 **Don't** think you are the only one. There are large numbers of incompetent people in top jobs within Britain plc. Many eventually get paid huge sums to go away. 'The higher up you are, the easier it is to get away with it,' says Sandi Mann, occupational psychologist at Salford University.

2 **Understand** that if you work for a rotten company, you are probably expected to be rotten, too. There are dysfunctional companies, just as there are dysfunctional families.

3 **Accept** that, if you have a varied career, you will probably find your limitations at some stage. The experience is a useful one to have when young. An 18-year old who was a terrible waitress can view the rest of her career as a wonderful escape. But many people find their weaknesses later on in life, as workers are expected to perform a broader range of functions in many jobs. Other workers have had to take over parts of a middle manager's role, for instance, as thousands of these employees have been made redundant.

4 **Realise** that you have four main options: bluffing your way through; training to improve your performance; finding someone else to take on some of your duties; and moving to a different job. The best way to bluff is often to choose a marvellous secretary and very efficient subordinates. Former consultant Mark Jarvis says, 'If you surround yourself by good people, you can get a reputation just for that. Colleagues can start to say: "Old so-and-so may not be the brightest, but he sure knows how to pick a team."' Training can make up for certain inadequacies – being scared to speak in public, for instance, or having no experience of management. But if you are terrified of figures and have to prepare complicated budgets, training may not help. You might be able to get someone else to help, or you might go for a change of job. More sophisticated employers will admire your honesty if you say something like: 'I feel my real strengths lie in the design field, and I would rather concentrate on them than on buying IT systems.'

5 **Make** sure you stay on friendly terms with people who may have influence. Many dullards survive simply because of the loyalty of colleagues. Bosses may ask, 'What's the point in getting rid of Fred? He's only got two years to retirement, and the staff would be upset if we sacked him now.'

6 **Don't** think that you will automatically be protected by your intelligence or training. The most spectacular example of this is probably the Lord Chancellor, Lord Irvine. He may be a great legal brain, but his performance in the profession's top job has so far been in some people's opinion a public-relations disaster.

How to avoid being stabbed in the back

1 **Recognise** your enemies. Most back-stabbers fall into one of two categories: the envious, who will take a personal dislike to you; and the ruthlessly ambitious, who look for fall-guys in difficult times. (There are also a few honourable assassins in the Brutus mould.) Talented, committed people are particularly at risk. Harriet Peters (not her real name) was recruited to her company's high-fliers promotion scheme only to be suspended from work when, on a four-day company tour, she used the company car for a five-mile private drive. 'If you are a mediocrity in a barrel of mediocrities, you can carry on happily being mediocrities together,' she says. 'But if you have ideas, you must not offend orthodoxies until your back is inviolate.'

2 **Watch** out for the usual warning signs. If you are slapped on the back by someone you don't trust, put yourself on red alert. Most people miss the signs and find out too late.

3 **Obey** company rules to the letter. Some back-stabbers are expert at getting people sacked for minor infringements.

Even if you work an extra hour at night, you are vulnerable if you arrive five minutes late in the morning. Never overclaim a penny on expenses.

4 **'Cultivate** the people above your tormentor,' says Ms Peters. 'Write memos to cover your position. If you are good at it, you can implicate people in the memos. Make sure that, if you have to go, your enemies go down with you.' Memos can prove that you took all the correct procedures and consulted your bosses. Envious back-stabbers may not be so well organised.

5 **Interpret** the meaning of silence and confusion. By definition, back-stabbers can operate only out of your line of vision. If you are an intelligent person and cannot understand what is happening in your workplace, you may have good reason to start feeling nervous.

6 **Understand** that back-stabbers are usually emotionally unstable and that you can sometimes beat them at their own game. Great politicians thrive on periods of prolonged uncertainty.

7 **Be** wary of unexpected invitations. Machiavelli's hero, Cesare Borgia, made a habit of throwing parties and murdering selected guests.

8 **Develop** contingency plans for finding a new job or a new role. In a climate of fear, there may be few survivors. Leaving the back-stabbers is often easier than you think. Ms Peters' next employers saw her previous problems as a recommendation – rather like a dishonourable discharge from the SS. Twenty-nine per cent of middle managers believe it is unlikely, or very unlikely, that their employer will keep promises made about their career, according to the Institute for Employment Studies. Most of today's businesses are 'highly political environments', according to research published by the Institute of Personnel and Development.

• •

How to blow the whistle

1 **Recognise** that whistle-blowing is a hard occupation. Whistle-blowers can get ostracised or sacked. Many people blow the whistle when they start a new job: it is particularly hard psychologically to finger long-standing colleagues.

2 **Consider** where you draw the line. Whistle-blowing is usually associated with financial fraud or health and safety, but there are growing concerns about such other areas as the abuse of old or vulnerable people in residential homes. Christina Toft of consultancy Merlin Development says abuse of the elderly is 'much more widespread than people realise'.

3 **Collect** your evidence carefully if you suspect wrongdoing. Many whistle-blowers are accused of conducting vendettas. Make notes of conversations and keep copies of relevant documents. 'Think through the possibilities that there could be an innocent explanation,' says a spokesman for the advice organisation Public Concern at Work.

4 **Be** very careful about taking documents home. 'Documents are the property of the company,' says Public Concern. 'If it is sensitive information, it could be seen as stealing or a breach of confidentiality.'

5 **Take** advice early. Public Concern at Work (tel. 0171-404 6609) gives free advice and, in its capacity as an independent lawyer, can look after documents for you.

6 **Try** to sort out your concerns with your employer first. See whether you can speak confidentially to someone senior in the organisation who could investigate your allegations. Should your employers not respond positively, however, you may need to go to such outside agencies as the Health and Safety Executive if, for example, you are worried about dangerous machinery.

7 **Avoid** being drawn into any impropriety yourself. You can be blackmailed. One of the best ways for a wrong-doer to protect himself is to create an accomplice of someone who might otherwise have spoken out.

* *

How to cope with a catastrophe

1 **Understand** that you may respond better if you have thought beforehand about the possible consequences. People who have witnessed car crashes are often better at keeping a cool head in other emergencies.

2 **Evacuate** the area if there is physical danger. 'Very often people will be able to focus – but they won't be able to focus on the right things,' says Neal Courtney of disaster recovery adviser Imbach. 'If they have personal items on their desk which get broken, they can see it as a violation.' They may be more worried about the broken photograph of their children than the possibility that the ceiling is about to fall in.

3 **Expect** a wide range of unexpected responses from colleagues. Doormen sometimes take control while senior executives panic. But people who deal with daily crises – IT personnel or buildings and facilities managers – often react well to larger problems.

4 **Divide** jobs among yourselves if you are one of the group taking control – eg one person will contact the police, another will ring the insurer. Make sure people who want to help have something to do; they get anxious otherwise. Work as a team.

5 **Accept** that your life might be severely disrupted as the result of a catastrophe. The experience of fear cannot be reversed. You should consider counselling, particularly if you suffer nightmares, loss of concentration or other signs of anxiety. Many people not even in the area at the time the IRA bombed Manchester city centre in 1996 were counselled afterwards because they were so scared by what might have happened to them.

6 **Ask** your employer for counselling, time off and better contingency plans if necessary. Employment law provides little direct pressure on employers to be sympathetic in these circumstances, says Michael Burd of solicitors Lewis Silkin, but more and more companies are seeing 'the benefits of dealing positively with this kind of situation'.

7 Realise that your status in the company might be changed for ever by your short-term reactions. Prince Charles's reputation would undoubtedly have suffered had he shown fear during an apparent assassination attempt in Australia. Some people show deep, unacknowledged gifts. One building society employee realised she had a taste for adventure and changed her life completely after being held up by a gunman in her branch. She emigrated to France, where she set up her own business.

8 Get your firm to plan ahead, particularly if you are made a fire warden or disaster recovery co-ordinator. These people can be made scapegoats if things turn nasty.

9 Don't automatically sell any shares you may have in the company. Research from Templeton College, Oxford, concludes that 'catastrophes offer an opportunity for management to demonstrate their talent in dealing with difficult circumstances'. Businesses are either 'recoverers' or 'non-recoverers'. Share prices grew 5 per cent on average over 50 days for recoverer companies, and fell 15 per cent over a year for non-recoverers.

How to deal with bereavement

1 **Expect** most employers to be sympathetic about time off. 'Employers tend to be quite compassionate; it depends how close the relative was,' says employment solicitor Michael Burd. 'There isn't a standard period of leave, but I've never heard of it being an issue.' A few employers, of course, are mean. Cruse, the bereavement counselling service, has seen 'appalling' cases in which people have been sacked for taking time off or being unable to concentrate properly on their return.

2 **Do** keep your boss informed. He or she may be sympathetic, but needs to know how long you will be away.

3 **Don't** forget about work completely. It is a vital part of recovery for many people – and your income may be even more important in future. 'Sometimes people like to go back very quickly to get out of the place where they have been grieving,' says Susan Wallbank of Cruse.

4 **Understand** that you may, at times, find it hard to focus when you start work again or that, having expended so much emotional energy, you may feel exhausted. Some people are put off returning to work because they think they might cry in public. Think of somewhere discreet you can go – a café, a quiet room or toilet – if this happens, or seek out a sympathetic colleague. Most people will be understanding, but you will feel better if you can cry in quiet.

5 **Avoid** assuming that your colleagues do not care for you because they do not mention your bereavement. 'Be aware that others will find it difficult to deal with, in terms of embarrassment,' says Steve Manton, a consultant who used to run employee stress counselling schemes. 'People who have suffered themselves are better equipped because they know what it is like.' But many people will take their lead from you. They may ask you general questions about how you are, but will leave it for you to decide when and how much you want to talk.

6 **Recognise** that the death of a loved one can have a dramatic, permanent effect on your attitude to your job. 'It can make you re-evaluate the direction of your life and your values – particularly if the death was unexpected or premature,' says Manton.

7 **Organise** the signing of a condolence card if a colleague suffers a bereavement. As well as showing solidarity, it can save the colleague embarrassment when he or she returns to work. 'One of the difficulties of being in a big organisation is knowing who has heard and who hasn't,' says Wallbank. 'Signing a condolence card is a good way of passing the information around.' Cruse (tel. 0181-940 4818) has 200 bereavement counselling centres around the country. The Samaritans and local services also provide help.

Reacting to change

How to deal with a new corporate identity

1 Don't fool yourself into thinking this is a minor step. You may dislike the new pastel brochures and matching reception area and logo, but your marketing department believes this illustrates the soul of your company, and they have probably persuaded the chief executive to think the same.

2 Understand that feelings of irritation are probably shared. It is no coincidence that British Airways' £60 million redesign in 1997 was accompanied by a threat of strike action. 'Staff must have wondered why they were spending £60m on a redesign instead of on pay,' says corporate identity consultant Chris Ludlow.

3 Expect some changes in procedures and in 'corporate culture'. You might be given detailed instructions about how to answer the phone or write letters. 'It removes individual idiosyncrasies,' said one marketeer preparing to launch a change of corporate identity. 'You can get very strict guidelines about how to act, and these have to be policed.'

4 **Worry** if your bosses don't explain the changes to you. Their failure to do so means that they are clearly inept and may have been persuaded to pay thousands of pounds to an expensive consultancy.

5 **Work** out why the changes are happening. The real reasons will not be disclosed if they are bad. Dramatic changes are a sign of desperation. Better-organised companies recognise that both customers and employees are wary of change.

6 **Don't** despair if you hear a new uniform is in the offing. The choice is much wider these days, says Ludlow: 'People often get winter shoes and summer shoes, for example. Uniforms are becoming more common – but they are getting more fashion-related as a way of creating a feelgood factor among the staff.'

How to get the best out of relocation

1 **Don't** expect your company to relocate to an idyllic spot. Although individuals rate Oxford, Edinburgh and Bristol as favourite cities, bosses are more likely to consider London, Birmingham and Manchester, according to Black Horse Relocation.

2 **Make** sure you get considerable financial assistance if you are being asked to move house. About 75,000 employees a year get 'full assistance' from their companies, according to Hambro Countrywide Relocation (HCR). Another 300,000 get some help. Government departments are more likely to give the same package to everyone, regardless of rank, whereas companies will give preference to people with specialist skills and to senior staff. Many firms will pay smaller expenses if asked – for example, the cost of a couple of 'familiarisation visits'.

3 **Ask** your company or local Inland Revenue inquiry office about the tax consequences of any assistance you get. Up to £8,000 of expenses can be received tax-free.

4 **Understand** that you will probably be tied to the company if you take a relocation package. Many firms will force you to reimburse them if you leave within four years. But you should be heartened if you are looking for job security: the finance director will look foolish if he or she gives you a hefty subsidy and makes you redundant the year following.

5 **Consider** using a relocation agent if your company won't help you. The Association of Relocation Agents (01273 624455) has a list of 180 companies. But fees are high: up to £500 to hire a firm and up to 1.5 per cent of the house price if they help you find a home. These agents will give practical assistance – on schools, for instance, or on jobs for your spouse.

6 **Understand** that the move may be more dramatic for your partner than for you. 'Trailing spouses' often find it difficult to get work and frequently have to make compromises – working part-time, going freelance or changing occupation. Some large firms will consider taking on the partner as well, but not in the same department as you.

7 **Accept** that most people find it difficult to adapt. 'If you think it's going to be difficult, you get through it,' says Andrew Finney of HCR. 'And relocating internationally is 10 times more difficult than a domestic move.' HCR advises people to plunge into their new social milieu by, for instance, holding a housewarming party for neighbours. You might even end up getting closer to colleagues.

•

How to tell whether your company is going under

1 **Look** for the worst psychological sign – an inability to plan for the inevitable. Hundreds of businesses go this way each year, including law firms that ignore the developments of technology, insurance companies that neglect the growing demands of their customers, businesses in small markets that don't diversify, or any firm dependent on one client or supplier.

2 **Take** warning if your bosses stop giving you rational answers to sensible questions. A period of confusion precedes many human crises. People are often reluctant to articulate very bad news. Like politicians facing impossible questions, company bosses frequently become snappy when they get trapped in a corner.

3 **Don't** assume that your company will be safe just because there are clever people in the boardroom: they can be just as blinkered as anyone else. The Liberal Party's rapid decline at the start of the twentieth century after some 16 years in office is suggestive that even the best brains may ignore the dangers bearing down on them.

4 **Become** uneasy at signs of unnecessary ostentation. Many insolvency practitioners say that the death-knell sounds when the statue of the chairman goes up in the reception area. 'Or if he gets a knighthood or goes into the House of Lords, the decline starts soon after that,' says accountant Paul le Druillenec. 'He becomes so puffed up with his own self-importance that his eye comes off the ball. For small businesses, the sign could be fancy notepaper with four-colour printing. It's money wasted that could be cash in the bank.'

5 **Watch** for the financial signs of chronic complacency: the sidelining of the finance director, for example; a poor understanding of budgeting throughout the organisation; customers who gradually take longer and longer to pay their bills; and, particularly, any whiff of financial scandal.

6 **Look** out for a lack of enthusiasm on the shop floor through declining orders and morale. Keith Goodman of insolvency practitioners Leonard Curtis says the workers are often ahead of the bosses: 'You get the feeling they knew before the management. They will be saying, "Them upstairs didn't realise what was happening down here."'

7 Evaluate the bosses' ability to turn the business around. Goodman says, 'You get companies making redundancy packages without addressing the main problem, which is ensuring the product makes sufficient gross profit.'

8 Change jobs, if you can, to avoid the sapping effects of long-term decline. Decay can last for decades. President Mobutu Sésé Séko dragged down the people of Zaïre for more than 30 years, despite the fact that the country had some of the richest mineral resources in the world. When you cannot fight against history, your best chance is to leave.

· ·
How to survive a takeover or merger

1 Expect a period of prolonged uncertainty. Most takeovers produce some redundancies, and the most efficient companies get these out of the way within days. But – as in the Commercial Union–General Accident merger of 1998 – many employees have to wait months after the initial announcement to know their fate.

2 Ask your manager, personnel department and trade union for more information if you are not told enough.

Few companies understand that their employees get anxious if they are not kept informed. Your inquisitiveness should not be held against you if you are cheerful and polite.

3 **Try** to establish how likely you are to be fired. 'If you are in the head office of a company that is being taken over, you should be very worried,' says accountant Paul Le Druillenec. The outlook is similar if you are in an unproductive backwater or if the other firm has a better department in your sector. Don't believe that talent, conscientiousness or other personal attributes will protect you. Find ways to score points if you want to stay. 'Maintain a positive profile,' says outplacement consultant Andy Andrews.

4 **Get** yourself some free in-house training if you think you will be laid off. You need to decide whether to wait for the redundancy money or get another job quickly. But if you know you are going to be sacked, you might as well enjoy yourself. Le Druillenec – who has himself been made redundant three times – says, 'I have found it to be a very relaxing and liberating time.'

5 **Prepare** yourself for a shoot-out if you think you are being measured up against a counterpart in the other firm. Find ways to show your ability to your management and theirs. At your disposal are the usual office-politics tools: memos, new projects, praise from influential sources, an unprecedented and unending record of mounting success, etc.

How to act if your boss is fired

Work out the reasons behind the boss's departure. If cost-cutting was a factor, the same fate may await you. 'I've participated in cases where we have decided to look at everyone who earned more than £25,000,' says manager Reg Webb. 'Then, when the new bosses have taken over, we have let them weed out a few of the juniors.'

Understand that your own position could be in danger. Sometimes secondary sackings will follow almost immediately, but many new bosses postpone a decision until they can evaluate their staff. Those associated with the old regime are particularly vulnerable. Webb adds, 'If the only purpose of secretaries or PAs was to make the boss's tea or book his girlfriends for the weekend, they aren't going to last long.'

Avoid mentioning your old boss to your new boss. People who say, 'Well, we always did it this way under Mr Perkins' will go in the black book immediately. Don't go collecting money for the old boss's leaving present if the new boss might walk in.

Don't shun your old boss. 'You never know when they might prove useful in the future,' says Percy, who lost a senior colleague this way. 'It doesn't do any harm to send your condolences.'

5 Ask yourself how you can benefit. Can you expand your empire, get rid of parts of your job that you don't like or even apply for the new vacancy yourself?

6 Try to avoid obsequiousness with a new boss. More mature managers dislike it, and the best ones find it distasteful. By presenting yourself as generally flexible and open-minded, you can achieve the same aims in a more subtle way. If crawling is necessary, it is a strong sign that the new boss is insecure and that further problems lie ahead.

7 Remember that first impressions are often wrong. Don't trust strangers too quickly: most ogres can smile for a few meetings. But after a few weeks they get tired of being nice and will start to show their true nature.

How to deal with the recruitment of a team

1 Accept that, generally speaking, team recruitment will happen more frequently – in the City, the law and elsewhere. It used to be frowned on by law firms, for example, as poaching but is now 'culturally acceptable' according to Mary Heaney, editor of *The Lawyer*: 'The arrival of American firms in London started the whole thing.' In an increasingly insecure job market, employees put more emphasis on money than on old-fashioned loyalty.

Prepare for a rough ride if a team is about to arrive in your department. 'As with football managers, it becomes an issue about turf and territory,' says psychologist Michael Carroll of consultancy Right Cavendish. 'The people arriving often expect the others to clear out – or they may keep them on, but as second-class citizens.' Unless the company makes a major effort to bridge the gap between old and new staff, there will inevitably be problems. Psychotherapist Frances Wilks of City University says, 'The arrival of groups can make people feel quite threatened – unless the employers do a lot of work to explain what it's about. It can be rather like guestworkers arriving from another country.'

Expect to find the company of your new colleagues difficult at the start. To justify the destabilisation of their arrival, they will be under considerable pressure to make major changes. They are likely to jettison useful as well as outdated procedures and systems. And the fact that they travel in groups could have other psychological meanings. Says Carroll: 'It could be they are insecure about what they do and find it too risky to go into the new situation on their own.'

Examine your own contract of employment if you are considering changing jobs as part of a team. If your present employer could also lose clients because of your departure, you could be subject to legal action. Some employers have been trying to force suspensions of up to a year on staff departing in this way. Like 'superwoman mother of five' and investment specialist Nicola Horlick, when she was suspended from Morgan Grenfell in January 1997, you could find yourself paid to do nothing.

5 **Understand** that the emergence of travelling teams in your industry could be the sign of other changes ahead. Management consultant David Temporal of Hodgart Temporal believes the law will be 'a very different profession' in a few years: 'Loyalty has diminished in many practices – particularly because of what people have been through. People want to reach their earning potential earlier.'

Relating to other people

How to be popular with colleagues

1 Always say hello in the morning. You cannot be popular with people whose existence you don't acknowledge.

2 Ask people about themselves, but in a probing, rather than factual, way. 'It almost invariably works,' says public relations specialist David Evans. 'Get them to discuss areas where they can teach you something. Ask them about what they are doing, their professional interests and techniques.'

3 Re-examine your own conversational habits. BT, which has extensively researched the issue of spoken communications, estimates that 'six out of 10 people in the UK want to be better communicators'. Impersonal, vague comments may sound polite, but are less absorbing than direct and specific remarks.

4 Avoid pointing the finger at other people, even when they are in the wrong. Colleagues will rapidly see you as the bringer of blame and recrimination. 'Crotchety people don't do as well as others,' says accountant Paul Le Druillenec. 'If you're a pain, nobody wants you in their team and you won't get on unless you are Beethoven.'

Be cheerful. Depressives are often kind at heart, but tend to feel lonely. People who don't appear to take life too seriously are often regarded as a burst of sunlight by colleagues. And remember to thank people.

Develop relationships with all your fellow workers, not just the influential or those in the same department. 'Never be arrogant with the people who keep places going,' says a House of Commons researcher. 'Porters, attendants and messengers can make life difficult if they want to.'

Decide to be helpful. Show people articles they might be interested in, take telephone messages for colleagues, and join the tea-making rota.

Avoid old-fashioned grovelling, but remember that while you don't have to call people 'sir' any more, few bosses like being told in public that they are fools.

Interpret feedback. Very popular people often have nicknames, know a great deal about their colleagues and can give advice about handling difficult situations, but they are often underpromoted. Many successful people appear friendly but keep a slight distance.

How to deal with colleagues from abroad

1 Be aware that misunderstandings occur when people are speaking a second language, even if they *sound* fluent. They may say, for example, that they are 'annoyed' when they mean 'surprised'.

2 Set aside extra time. 'Don't dismiss an extended social lunch as an outdated, time-wasting Latin tradition,' says Chris Crosby, who runs cross-cultural training programmes for consultants TMA. Getting to know potential business partners is a crucial prelude to doing the business in some cultures. Allow half an hour at the end of a meeting for unscheduled topics.

3 Recognise that the brisk British approach is often misread by other traditions. Someone who reads a proposal and says bluntly, 'So how will you achieve this?' may be seen as implying that the suggestion cannot work.

4 Avoid irony: it is inappropriate in some cultures. Former diplomat Ernest Clarke says, 'I get on very well with Ludwig, but for the first 10 years he didn't realise I was pulling his leg. Then he realised, and for the next year fell about laughing whenever I spoke; even my most serious remarks were taken that way.'

5 Take care with meetings. Tell everyone to turn up promptly if you wish them to do so. Continentals are likely to assume a meeting billed to start at 3 pm will start at 3.15.

Look out for body language that indicates someone is struggling. Use oral, written and visual communication to give your message a range of ways to get through. Crosby says, 'People from the Mediterranean are ready to act on the spoken word. Others will not take the spoken word seriously unless it is in writing.'

Don't read too much into the way people dress. A well-dressed Italian might appear in a smart blazer and slacks when a Briton would wear a suit.

- -

How to shake hands or kiss people

Understand that handshaking and particularly kissing are seeing a resurgence in popularity in the warm and caring 1990s businessworld. But the motives may not be pure, says psychologist Michael Carroll of consultancy Right Cavendish: 'People often like to rush a relationship: the quicker you can seem to be close friends, the better it is for the marketing business.'

Stick to handshaking unless you are confident the other person wants to be kissed. Many people – such as husband and wife politicians Peter and Virginia Bottomley – would never kiss their nearest or dearest in public. Although combatants may shake hands (like boxers touching gloves before a fight), people who kiss are usually allies – hence the controversy over Judas Iscariot.

3 **Resist** the temptation to prove your virility in handshakes: it often backfires. John Major is a well-known bone-crusher. 'You can't do anything about it,' says someone who still nurses the memory of his grip. 'His was so firm it hurt.' Carroll says, 'People who give these handshakes may think "See how strong my handshake is – I'm like this in the rest of my life." But I interpret it as "See how insensitive my handshake is – I'm like this in the rest of my life."'

4 **Decide** beforehand on your handshaking policy. You make yourself look indecisive if you vaguely proffer your hand. In the UK, people rarely shake hands with colleagues after the first introduction. Life is different on the Continent where, says Brendan Donnelly MEP, 'It's almost impossible to shake hands too often.' Chancellor Kohl and his former foreign minister Hans Dietrich Genscher used to shake hands each day.

5 **Recognise** the ambivalent reaction you get for a two-handed shake or if you also put your left hand on the other person's elbow. Frances Cook, managing director of human resource consultancy Sanders & Sidley gives talks on physical presentation and regularly uses the double-handed 'Cherie Booth shake': 'This warm clasp is suitable for someone you know well or someone you feel enormously warm towards but don't know very well.' But former civil servant Keiron suspects fake intimacy from these holds: 'I can't believe that someone I've just met can feel so deeply about me.'

6 **Work** out your kissing policy beforehand, if you decide to go down that route. Cook kisses all the members on her board, for example. Selective kissing of some colleagues can promote envy. Kissing on the cheeks is safer than the fully frontal approach. If you are a known hugger, certain people will make a bee-line for you. 'I had someone kiss me yesterday that I'd never seen before,' says Gladys, a researcher.

7 **Try** to be sincere: not much goodwill is exuded when Aunt Ethel holds up her cheek for you to kiss. There are bigger dangers, perhaps, at the other end of the spectrum. Kisser *extraordinaire*, politician Mo Mowlam, often grappled with Unionists in Northern Ireland who were desperate to get away.

8 **Remember** that unless you work in the theatre or are a paid-up member of the Mafia, male-to-male kissing will only get you into trouble. (But bear in mind that among, for example, Southern Europeans it is quite acceptable for men to kiss each other on both cheeks – see 'How to deal with colleagues from abroad', pages 93–4.)

How to conduct an office romance

1 Keep your relationship quiet in the first stages, especially if it is shaky. Romances between equals attract gossip, but if one of the people involved is in a senior position, the relationship can also inspire jealousy and distrust.

2 Check your employment terms for an 'anti-dating clause'. Some UK employers are following this US fashion, says James Davies of solicitors Lewis Silkin: 'Dating can lead to sexual-harassment problems for the employer if the relationship breaks down.' Some employers will transfer one partner or spouse to another branch or department.

3 Consider telling your boss. 'If the relationship is going to become known – which it will do – it's far better to get in first,' says Jo Bond of Coutts Career Consultants. Say that it won't affect your work but that you wanted to let the boss know. You may decide against coming clean if your boss is unsympathetic, the affair is illicit or you are gay and working in a narrow-minded company.

4 Maintain faithfully your duties of confidentiality, particularly if you have access to such sensitive information as accounts or salaries. Accountant Paul Le Druillenec, who specialises in the media, says, 'Lots of people get very fussed at the idea of anyone in an office having sex with anyone. But in TV companies it seems to happen all the time. I just tell people that absolute confidentiality is required, and if they breach it they are fired.'

5 **Try** to move to a different department if your relationship could cause competitive problems. Affairs between bosses and secretaries are less threatening than relationships between a manager and a member of a large team. A junior partner promoted by their lover can be seen as a Mata Hari.

6 **Never** flaunt your relationship on office premises, either by kissing in the corridor or by discussing the colour of your kitchen units. Err on the side of formality. MPs Virginia and Peter Bottomley only shake hands in public.

7 **Demonstrate** your independence from each other to remind colleagues of your professionalism. The occasional disagreement over points of principle can be useful.

8 **Avoid** the allure of secret assignments and communications. Naughty e-mails have a habit of going astray.

• •
How to come out if you are gay

1 **Resist** the temptation, in most circumstances, to come out strongly on your first day. Very confident people can manage it; others will be stereotyped. 'Give yourself time to establish your personality,' says Jo, a journalist. 'Do you want the label "journalist" or "police officer", or do you want "lesbian"?' A 1993 survey by lobbying group Stonewall found that only 30 per cent of gay people were out with everyone at work.

2 Consult friends outside work, and choose a time when you feel happy. 'It is nerve-wracking, even if you get a brilliant reception,' says Jo. 'If you present a confident face, it will make others comfortable.' Come out 'slowly' with trusted colleagues, suggests administrator Eoin. Like Angela Eagle MP, whose coming out as the first lesbian parliamentarian was welcomed by Tony Blair, you are more likely to get a good reception if your boss is supportive.

3 Understand that a workplace that would have potentially been hostile a couple of years ago might have changed. 'People have far less expectation of a "normal" married relationship,' says public relations consultant Simon. 'It's moved on, in many places, from shock, hushed voices and people saying "Homo-what?"' Even so, many people have horrific experiences. One woman was accepted by all her colleagues except the person she shared an office with. She lost her job and nearly had a nervous breakdown. 'It takes only one person to make it a problem,' says a spokeswoman for Stonewall.

4 Recognise that the news could spread quickly. If you expect some hostility, you can let it be known that you are happy to discuss the subject.

5 Work out in advance what you will do if people ask awkward questions. Gay men are often thrown into a dilemma when someone in the photocopier queue asks, 'So, when you went to Devon last weekend, was that with your girlfriend?' You may be happy to tell them the truth, but may equally not want to announce it in this fashion to the other 15 people you work with.

6 Brace yourself for some embarrassing experiences. Simon says, 'You can find yourself pushed forward, with the black person and the Jew, as an example of how open-minded your company is.'

7 Capitalise on a positive reception by trying diplomatically to improve your workplace rights. Some companies will give pensions to gay partners, but they may need encouragement. Laws on this could change rapidly. The European Court of Justice may have given a negative response in 1998 to the application of lesbian railway worker Lisa Grant to be treated on a par with heterosexual couples and get a travel pass for her girlfriend, but most employment lawyers believe that moral pressure will lead to rapid improvements for the gay community at work.

••

How to cope if your boss doesn't like you

1 Accept that your happiness could be blighted and promotion prospects blocked unless you do something. Don't spend your life hating someone: Sergeant Reegan in

John McGahern's *The Barracks* ruins his life by becoming fixated with his boss, 'the bastard Quirke'.

2 **Work** out whether your boss is basically reasonable. Perhaps *you* are the difficult one. 'Study [your boss's] relationships with others,' says former teacher Beverly Bond. 'We all have things that irritate us intensely but don't bother other people.' If everyone hates the boss, there may be little you can do, except look for a transfer. But you may have touched a funny bone. They may have a particular grouch, or a chip on the shoulder – such as a worry that a high-flier of your calibre will end up stealing their job.

3 **Take** responsibility, says human resource consultant Tom Barry. 'Don't wait for them to come to you. Nowadays bosses tend to manage 10 to 15 people, so they aren't sitting there worrying about you.'

4 **Ask** your boss, suggests Barry, to list the 10 most important skills for your job. Prepare your own list beforehand. You can then see the difference. Don't ask your boss to comment on you personally. Many people would clam up and might get angry.

5 **Work** out what you can do to make their life easier. People are more often liked for the small extra things they do – covering up the mistakes of colleagues, for instance – than for fulfilling their job description.

6 **Accept** that many bosses are promoted for technical ability and lack personal skills. Many insurance companies are run by introverted actuaries – not usually the best motivators of others. You may be only a 19-year-old filing clerk, but your communication skills could be much better than theirs. 'Make them feel at ease,' says Bond. 'Ask questions and learn from them. Everybody likes it if you do that.'

7 Have a frank discussion, if you think they will respond. 'It should be a bit like couples counselling,' says occupational psychologist Sandi Mann of Salford University. 'You're not accusing them, just saying how you feel.' Instead of asking 'Why did you tell me off publicly?', you could say, 'I felt embarrassed in front of the others.'

8 Advertise successes. If your boss is impressed by brasher colleagues, you need to box clever. Avoid overt bragging, but you could ask, for instance, whether they have any particular expectations for the new client relationship you have established.

9 Understand that, in some cases, your poor relationship is a sign that your boss simply does not want you around. Accountant Paul Le Druillenec says, 'One reason why centralised human resource departments are such a bad idea is that they can recruit unsuitable people and then dump them on department heads.'

How to work in a one-to-one relationship

1 **Understand** that good relationships are vital, not just desirable. 'You have to make it your business to get on,' says Michael about his relationship with his secretary. 'Both of you need to feel that you will be defended by the other.' Another of his assistants did her job adequately but didn't fight his corner on two crucial occasions; they parted company.

2 **Spend** time observing and getting to know each other. 'That doesn't mean slapping them on the back, but bothering to get to know them and what they like,' says Sandy, a small-businesswoman. You need to win their respect because your failings will be particularly conspicuous. Someone who works in a large company can camouflage their mistakes – because no one knows how they spend every minute.

3 **Accept** that the balance of power is likely to change over time. A new assistant is expendable if he or she gets things wrong; an experienced one can be the power behind the throne. Former Conservative MP Neil Hamilton met his future wife when she worked as his secretary; in time Christine Hamilton became regarded as the more formidable of the two. And the source of power in Daphne Du Maurier's *Rebecca* clearly lay with the housekeeper.

4 **Keep** on trying to impress the other, and renegotiate terms. Both parties need to ensure that the junior one does not feel too anxious to set out his or her desired conditions and boundaries. Like a marriage, the relationship can go stale if you don't work at it. Michael says, 'The employee is well advised to keep brushing up their skills. If they can say that they have taught themselves e-mail, for instance, that keeps the interest going.'

5 **Expect** to get lonely sometimes. Try to meet other people who have a similar role. The Transport and General Workers' Union started a newsletter in 1998 for 200 MPs' researchers and secretaries. 'The job can be very isolating, as we stick in our offices and each individually re-invent the wheel,' wrote researcher Gary Kent in the first issue. 'But there are ways of meeting other people and sharing skills.'

6 **Look** for another job if you get on badly. Many people submit to a slave-and-master relationship for years – think of the character Baldrick in Rowan Atkinson's television series *Blackadder*. Bosses can get into the habit of attacking the only people who will put up with their abuse – their assistants.

7 **Don't** be surprised if you start to use each other's phrases and gestures. Many people in this situation start to copy each other's behaviour – in the tradition of the dog and master who look more like each other as they get older.

How to avoid office civil war

1 **Recognise** the signs early. Allegations over minor matters, the spread of suspicion and rumour, the rise of fanatics and the declining influence of stable characters, a loss of perspective and a failure to concentrate on the job in hand all indicate your workplace is on the verge of a witch hunt or civil war.

2 **Establish** a clear system of justice that rewards sensible behaviour. The Salem witch hunts of 1692 systematically encouraged people to suppress the truth and make false accusations – a form of irrationality that can quickly spread in the workplace. Extremists always shout the loudest, but you need to encourage the prudent majority who abide by the rules. Never believe that obsessives will become reasonable if you appease them: they usually want more.

3 **Try** to limit the damage if you believe some pain is necessary. A fight is fairer if it has a time limit, a referee and a set of rules. The 1997 battle for the Conservative party leadership was particularly gruelling because it had no agreed parameters.

4 **Understand** that in-fighting thrives in an atmosphere of secrecy and injustice. Many slave rebellions in the West Indies were undermined by slaves who felt they had less to lose personally by betraying their colleagues than by participating. Simple measures can be taken to restore an atmosphere of openness. Former administrator

Melanie O'Hara says, 'You can create suspicion just by going into the boss's office, closing the door, staying there for 10 minutes and coming out looking sly. But you create an atmosphere of greater openness if you leave the door open.'

5 Never become abusive. You lose your credibility if you appear to lose your objectivity. Liberal Democrat party leader Paddy Ashdown always had a head start over former Prime Minister John Major in explaining policy because he never made personal or emotive comments about 'bastards', 'boys' or 'belly-fulls'.

6 Recognise that civil war is a necessary part of change in organisations that have been unable to set up a more sophisticated mechanism for development. 'You can't do away with in-fighting,' says O'Hara. 'In fact, I always enjoyed a certain amount of plotting myself.'

• •

How to survive office feuds

1 Look out for the defining characteristics of feuds – frustration on both sides, persistence and an excuse. 'It's a very overblown form of sibling rivalry which has gone on far beyond its sell-by date,' says psychotherapist Frances Wilks of City University. 'Children compete for the best things – father's attention or the biggest ice cream. If they don't resolve the situation when they are younger, the jockeying for position carries on in later life.'

2 Expect most feuds to be between colleagues of similar rank who cannot easily be fired. The 10-year fight between the dean and sub-dean of Lincoln Cathedral could not be resolved by outside intervention because neither man could be sacked. It was only when the dean retired that the financial disputes and other squabbles came to an end. The hierarchy of the public sector has also been a breeding ground for disputes: the allocation of car-parking spaces, elaborate job titles and other minor perks give great scope for envy.

3 Stay out of it unless you have heard the story from many sides and are sure it is worth getting involved. Spouses, relatives and friends all become targets in feuds – rather as in Mafia wars. Becky was marked down in her university finals because of her admiration for her professor: 'You might think that you are just making one friendship – but actually you are joining an army. 'The other lot immediately sees you as completely unreliable and writes you off.'

4 Consider trying to mediate – but only if you have something to gain. The warring parties have persistence and several other traits in common – and may well unite in despising you. Such people – the Reverend Ian Paisley, for instance – tend to see themselves as principled and uncompromising; they often see potential peacemakers as weak. An astute boss may be able to negotiate a compromise – probably by pointing out the damage done to the individuals as well as to the company. Don't get dragged into the details, says Wilks. 'You'll get into endless cycles of blame – "She pulled my hair first" and so on. You've got to cut your way through that.'

5 **Accept** that reconciliation is not always in your interests. Prime Minister Tony Blair has surrounded himself by people who dislike each other but are loyal to him. 'If you can keep on good terms with both sides, you are in a very strong position,' says another politician. 'You can call for support from both – but they are locked in a dance of death and have to disagree with each other at every opportunity.'

• •
How to deal with an unstable colleague

1 **Understand** that although workplace stress is becoming commonplace, people react very differently to identical pressures. Most people react badly to the threat of job loss, demotion or a pay cut. But someone who relishes a tight deadline may crumble under the burden of tough sales targets. As many as one in four people suffers from some form of mental health problem in their life – and most people frightened of losing their jobs go through prolonged emotional upheaval.

2 **Look** out for the classic signs: an unexpected increase in irritability, poor concentration, loss of sense of humour, mood swings, fear verging on paranoia, heavy drinking, feelings of incompetence and unworthiness or workaholism. But be careful: the fact that someone hears voices may be a sign of schizophrenia. However, according to the mental health charity Mind many people hear voices throughout their lives without any harmful effects. It could be more worrying if a usually efficient colleague takes an hour to decide whether to take a bus or a taxi.

3 **Sound** the person out – in a gentle chat if you are a colleague or in an informal appraisal session if you are the boss. Former administrator Anita Patel says, 'Do the agony-aunt bit, but don't end up nurturing a lunatic.'

4 **Consider** whether there are organisational changes you could make to help your colleague. If you notice the signs early, you may be able to reorganise his or her job slightly. Those incapable of saying no may need protection from colleagues who load them down. Gregarious characters will become depressed if forced to work in isolation.

5 **Discuss** the situation with your superiors or with personnel if you remain concerned. Steve Manton of M Pire, a consultancy that advises stress counselling schemes, says, 'The consequences can be very serious if the person is in a high position.' Peter Young, the fund manager at the heart of the Morgan Grenfell crisis, appears to have been left largely to his own devices, despite the fact that colleagues were concerned about his eccentric behaviour. Young's wife became alarmed when he went to do the family shopping and returned with 30 jars of pickled gherkins, but nothing else.

6 **Resist** any good intentions to do too much. Although you should try to ensure that the problem is addressed, you are unlikely to be the person best suited to giving that help. Serious problems should be treated by professionals – usually counsellors and doctors. A guide published by Mind says that it is sometimes 'simply impossible' for people to open up to their relatives (let alone colleagues): 'People who have had similar experiences are often the easiest to communicate with.' (*How to Recognise the Early Signs of Mental Distress*, Mind Publications, 15–19 Broadway, Stratford, London E15 4BQ; £1.00 with a 31p SAE. For information on mental health services ring the Mind information line on 0345 660163.)

• •

How to avoid those embarrassing moments in the lift

1 **Recognise** that the easiest way to survive those awkward moments in the lift is to stare at your shoes. Tall buildings provide the greatest potential for embarrassment. 'Lift journeys can go on a long time,' says an old hand from London's 42-storey NatWest Tower. 'Don't start a conversation if you can't sustain it for three minutes.'

2 **Don't** be inhibited, however, if you have the social skills to become a 'lift character'. You will need at least one of the following: a gift for one-liners and repartee, a reliable memory for names or a warm and vibrant personality. 'People who do not behave according to the normal rules in lifts are deeply loved,' says Gladys, a former Civil

Servant who rose to become an expert in lift psychology. 'Someone who bounds in and beams can have an extraordinary effect in 10 seconds.'

3 **Insist** on the highest standards of 'lift etiquette'. It is a sad company where everyone has to push the button themselves: the person nearest the controls should act as lift operator.

4 **Remember** that careless talk in lifts can cost you your reputation. Never chatter in front of people you do not recognise – particularly if you are travelling to the higher floors, where the senior management usually resides. The NatWest lift expert warns: 'Never indulge in office gossip, because the person you are speaking about will get in at the next floor. It all then becomes very obvious if you have several people trying to maintain a silence.'

5 **Cast** off your atavistic feelings of anxiety at being in this enclosed space. You could use the few minutes to clear your mind. Or, if you want to be more active, you could practise pulling in your stomach or buttock muscles. No one else will notice, unless you are wearing very tight clothes.

6 **Remember** that when you bump into the top dogs in the lift, they probably feel more nervous than you do. You may well know a lot about them, whereas they are probably trying to recall what your name is. Bowing and scraping is probably the most common response to bosses, but other approaches can be deeply refreshing. One particularly extrovert cleaning lady at the Department of

Trade and Industry head office in the 1980s used to greet Lord Tebbit with comments like 'Taking a half-day, then?'

● ●

How to break bad news

Resist the temptation to soften the blow with gracious words. Get to the point: 'As you know, the company has been scaling back its activities, and I am sorry to say that your job is redundant.' Saying first how much a person is valued sends misleading signals. Statements like 'You can now spend more time watching Arsenal' will only anger people. 'You're trying to build in a positive side for someone who hasn't yet dealt with the negative,' says psychologist Michael Carroll of consultancy Right Cavendish.

Check that the person has understood. People's absorption rates differ. Suppress your emotions: imagine how surprised you would be to see an emotional newscaster on television.

Accept that the other person will feel vulnerable. Have a plan to help restore his or her dignity. 'People feel out of control temporarily when they get bad news,' says Rosemary Edgar of Coutts Career Consultants. 'Make sure they get back as much control as possible. Give them the choice of what to do next.' Someone whose main project is cut might want to get back to his or her desk immediately, take an early lunch, or discuss the facts with somebody else.

4 **Make** sure that bad news is discussed in private, where possible. Don't get defensive if people get angry. They will become calmer if you say things like 'I can understand why you feel this way.' But defensive justifications ('Well, if you want to know, we decided not to promote you because you are too old') will just make matters worse.

5 **Ensure** that people will be safe when they leave you. Many recipients of unwelcome news will get comfort from being with others. They won't have a source of sympathy if you tell them as everyone else is going home. Avoid delivering bad news on Friday evenings, or just before a holiday. Don't let someone drive home if they are in shock.

6 **Give** people a few moments' warning in situations where they need to maintain composure. One of Margaret Thatcher's advisers used to whisper 'Good news' or 'Bad news' as ministers involved in Cabinet reshuffles were called in to see her.

7 **Understand** that the announcement of a disaster – your own sacking or President's Kennedy's death – will be remembered in detail for years. You may never be forgiven if you handle it badly.

How to deal with auditors

1 Resist paranoia. Detailed inquiries about your work are part of a standard audit. Auditors usually try to look at different parts of a company's business each year. If they ask why you do not have receipts for expenses, they are probably more concerned about your employer's records than about you.

2 Be helpful. The people doing the fieldwork are probably juniors. You can make their lives miserable by leading them up the garden path, but it could rebound if they get the wrong end of the stick.

3 Chat to them. They will have an insight into the health of your company that you do not have. Even throw-away remarks – 'Your company takes far longer to audit than the others we deal with' – can be revealing.

4 Avoid criticising your superiors to the auditors. It could get back to them. Auditors may be good with figures, but they are not known for their skill with words or diplomacy.

5 Consider this an ideal opportunity for stirring things up. A few casual words about another department could get the auditors out of your hair and into theirs.

6 Don't fret if they find a mistake. Decent employers will understand. Accountant Paul Le Druillenec regularly works with auditors: 'I always tell my staff that they should not be upset if the auditors find a mistake. It's quite hard to get your work right all the time.'

7 **Understand** that auditors are naturally conservative. Their main aim is to keep your company's business. They may look unpleasant but they rarely look for blood. Remember – Barings, BCCI, the Maxwell empire and a host of other interesting companies always got clean audit reports. Only 2 per cent of frauds are discovered by the company's auditors, according to the fraud unit of accountants Ernst & Young.

How to deal with management consultants

1 **Don't** blab. A visit from management consultants often precedes redundancies. Consultant Alan Hodgart of Hodgart Temporal says, 'If someone feels uncomfortable with the questions they are being asked, they should give the answers they think are appropriate. Why should you stick your neck out unless you can trust the people you are speaking to?'

2 **Make** sure you give the impression of being helpful. Management consultants often make comments to the bosses on particular individuals. Accountant Paul Le Druillenec has dealt with consultants in the past and says, 'Make it seem that you are privy to lots of dark secrets that can't be handed out. This enhances one's status. But don't be too helpful, because they are there to do you out of a job.'

3 **Consider** the political implications of the consultants' appointment. Consultants are often called in to sort out a crisis on the board. They often act as the bearers of bad news when the board is too squeamish to do the job alone. They could even be undercover accountants doing diligence work for a takeover.

4 **Find** out exactly who appointed the consultants. Like politicians with referendums, directors rarely call in consultants unless they believe they will like the outcome.

5 **Decide** whether the consultants have come to downsize or with a more positive purpose. If you can't work out the reason, it could well be downsizing. Hodgart says: 'The biggest problem is that management often aren't trusted, and people don't know the truth about why the consultants are there. If they are there to downsize, management will never tell people that.' If the reason is not to do with downsizing, and you trust your employers and the consultants, you can speak more freely.

6 **Be** particularly careful with junior consultants, who may not have much experience. They could mark you down on their check-lists as a potential troublemaker if you sound disrespectful of the high command.

7 **See** whether you can learn any new tricks from the consultants. They are increasingly being brought in for reasons other than redundancies. 'Most of the time we are looking at the strategy of organisations, business processes and how to implement technology,' says management consultant Vic Luck.

7 React with enthusiasm when you are told how to implement the consultants' conclusions. If your bosses have wasted the company's money in commissioning the report, they will not thank you for telling them so. Le Druillenec says, 'Appear to embrace the conclusions and to be entirely 100 per cent in favour of them – but don't move too quickly. The serious error is to say "That's silly" to a bad boss. Saying yes but not doing anything has saved me a lot of time.'

How to deal with the public

1 Understand that many people cannot cope with this kind of work. You may be one of them – if, for example, you can't bear repetition or don't enjoy observing human nature. Those most able in this role, like radio phone-in hosts, tend to have a positive view of human nature and often expect the best of people.

2 Smile, count to 10 and take the following old-fashioned advice if people are getting on your nerves: 'It makes an enormous difference if you smile as you speak,' says Civil Servant and former complaints-handler David. 'If you look interested and let them talk, people burn themselves out.'

3 **Never** take bad temper personally. 'People who are good at dealing with the public often have very strong boundaries and are usually very well worked out,' says psychotherapist Frances Wilks, personal development course director at City University. 'They have a great deal of empathy, but they don't take things personally. They understand that when someone is angry, they are not angry with them; it's just that life isn't working out that day.' If you deal with 100 people in a day, you will undoubtedly find some in a bad mood.

4 **Use** your imagination to think about the pressures faced by different clients. An elderly person who lives alone may want to be eased into a conversation with their bank manager by chatting about the weather – but a workaholic with a lunchtime appointment will get agitated by small talk.

5 **Don't** assume that ordinary people will lead their private lives as efficiently as you lead your work life. You may be employed to send out long letters explaining why people owe more tax. They will often be so shocked to receive the letter that they react emotionally rather than rationally. Many will not read the letter at all and might phone to ask you to explain. If you become impatient, you will be missing some important points about human nature.

6 **Look** for support from colleagues if you feel harassed. The better you are at the job, the more you may have sublimated your normal responses and need to express your frustration. The pressure will be particularly acute if you are under time constraints – perhaps having to make a lot of telephone calls in an hour. If you don't have someone to agree with you that 'that guy definitely sounds like a creep', you might get depressed and start blaming yourself. Many kind people have a tendency to blame themselves.

7 Savour the good moments. If you observed people closely, you would soon have material for a novel. 'People can say one sentence and you can construct so much of their whole situation from it,' says former postman Nick Gillies. Another postman's perk is 'seeing famous people in their dressing gowns'.

Improving communications

How to take criticism

Distinguish between positive comments aimed at helping you improve and those that drag you down. A constructive critic will say, 'That wasn't your best report, but you could improve it by doing x'. According to psychotherapist Frances Wilks of City University, London, 'The underlying sense is that they have great hopes for you and are helping you improve.' A negative critic is defeatist: 'You're just bad at writing.'

Evaluate the comments. Because the critic has spent time judging your behaviour, he or she probably has time to talk it through. Destructive comments that touch a soft spot, such as being told you dress frumpily when you are worried about your appearance, are particularly undermining.

Accept positive criticism as gracefully as you can – if you think it is true. The British respect those who take it on the chin. If you are really in a hole – for example, the final stages of a disciplinary procedure – a willingness to improve could make all the difference. Ask for more specific information if you aren't sure about the comments made.

4 Don't shout back if someone is abusive. You need to get that person onto a rational level. Sleep on it, talk to friends, try to work out why he or she was so angry. When you have regained your balance, you can tell your critic that what was said upset you, and can ask for specific suggestions on how to improve. Some people do not realise they are being rude – for example, the lofty boss who never gives praise but then criticises paragraph 93 in a long report.

5 Understand that adverse criticism is going out of fashion. In the days of more hierarchical workforces, bosses were almost expected to make withering comments; now, anyone doing this would be regarded as having a problem. 'If you are deeply critical, look at whether you are doing it as a way of not criticising yourself. There is often a displacement,' says Wilks. Happy people are rarely catty. Wilks suggests talking to a mentor and perhaps keeping a log of events to see common triggers.

6 Try to pre-empt giving or receiving destructive criticism by improving your communications with colleagues. 'Employers are now realising that they can't help people learn until they feel secure,' says psychologist Michael Carroll of consultancy Right Cavendish. 'You don't learn from bosses you don't like or respect.'

How to make a complaint

1 Remember that you can ruin your reputation by complaining formally about colleagues, even if justice is on your side. 'If the employee wants to prolong the relationship, they should think carefully about using the grievance procedure,' says employment solicitor Michael Burd. Local government is different: 'taking a grievance' can pass the time.

2 Recognise that, like most people, you are probably bad at complaining. 'When we get embarrassed we stop interacting in a normal way,' says psychotherapist and City University course director Frances Wilks. 'Talk to the person as a human being, not an object.' Explain the situation as equals rather than being plaintive.

3 Make sure that you have the facts. Many disputes are caused by misunderstandings. Instead of accusing someone of letting you down, you are usually best advised to start by saying: 'Fred, I think we are going about this project in different ways. How are you approaching it?' Those who get on best with colleagues rarely think in terms of making a complaint. They see the process as *clarification*.

4 Decide what you want before you go public. Many people get fixated on a particular problem and can spend years fighting for an apology. You are usually better off looking for a practical solution – a way of working that will stop the problem from recurring.

5 **Be** specific and keep notes. You make yourself look formidable and well-organised if you have written evidence, even if it is just your own record of events.

6 **Don't** get angry with the person handling your complaint. This is akin to blaming a judge in a court case. 'Anger is the wrong emotion,' says former ombudsman Adam Samuel. 'The complaint-handler is your ally; you persuade people by being reasoned, factual and persuasive.'

7 **Accept** that if you are constantly griping, the fault may lie with you. Perhaps you are the one who cannot do the job.

· ·
How to give advice to colleagues

1 **Avoid** giving advice directly. A small minority of people might be grateful, but most will see you as condescending. 'It's quite patronising to give advice straight off,' says psychotherapist Frances Wilks, personal development course director at City University. 'It makes people feel belittled and humiliated: it takes them back to a childhood role.' The phrase 'Let me give you a word of advice . . .' often precedes a savage attack.

2 **Understand** that giving advice is a risky business. Of course, you can sometimes have a dramatically positive effect: Ruth, a regular giver of advice, was recently told by a contact 'Thank you for telling me to pull my socks up two years ago. I listened, and my life has improved immeasurably.' But you will often fail, and be called bossy into the bargain. 'This is the problem that agony-aunt columns have,' says psychotherapist Michael Carroll of consultancy Right Cavendish. 'They are solving a problem rather than helping the person. Rather than giving an off-the-shelf answer, it is better to try to help the individual.'

Find ways of disguising your help. Your best contribution is often to encourage the other person to talk. 'It's always better if they can see the solution for themselves,' says Wilks. She once helped two rowing colleagues to make amends with each other. When she suggested that the company's administration systems were inadequate, they worked out a new way of running their affairs that minimised the friction.

Don't get too involved. Someone who is determined to make a disaster of their lives will not respond to helpful hints about meeting deadlines or having a clear-desk policy. Alcoholics, like the former executive in the film *Leaving Las Vegas*, often avoid people who tell them they drink too much.

Try to put yourself on an equal footing with the person you are helping. Women are often better than men at playing down their own achievements: they often say things like 'I've made so many mistakes myself, so I know what it's like.' Don't pick the day when the other person has announced his or her divorce and been demoted. 'People's reactions vary enormously,' says public relations consultant Michelle Lloyd-Jones, who regularly has to give advice to clients. 'It often depends on how much stress they are under that day.'

Look out for the odd person who is grateful for help. Young people or those who rarely get exposed to sharp analysis can find their lives transformed by some carefully chosen words. 'I'm still grateful to Max for telling me how to market myself 10 years ago,' says Margaret.

Use the modern alternatives to advice wherever you can. Customer feedback forms provide objective information that can be used as a basis for discussion and a reason for everyone in the department to change their procedures. The growing emphasis on training means that people can work on their weak spots before they get into trouble.

....

How to deal with people who are rude on the phone

Understand that people are more likely to be rude on the phone than face to face. About 65 per cent of employees admit to being rude in telephone calls, compared with 9 per cent in the flesh, says Reed Employment. Even people canvassing on the doorstep for political parties are usually impressed by the polite response they get. Anonymity and distance, on the other hand, make it easier to be nasty.

Accept that people are often rude under pressure. A former Royal Opera House director, Keith Cooper, was filmed picking up and slamming down a phone in the fly-on-the-wall television series *The House*.

Try to discern why someone is angry, even if you have to guess. You might blame yourself unnecessarily if you don't see other causes. Psychotherapist and City University course director Frances Wilks cites the example of a Civil Servant who suggested that a caller look up a number in a directory. He shouted back at her: 'I can't read, you dozy bitch.' 'It was so dreadful that she put the phone down,' said Wilks. 'But at least she did realise why he was being so rude.'

Never get angry back. Many confrontations are caused by a misunderstanding. 'The angrier and louder they become, the calmer you should remain,' says public relations consultant Michele Lloyd-Jones. If you are both angry, you will probably have a row. Even if you are blameless, you might feel upset afterwards and embarrassed in front of colleagues.

Understand that maintaining your calm is much easier than it sounds, but you must prepare by designing a strategy. Most call centres train staff in these techniques; other office workers have to train themselves. 'Be really, really nice back: it throws them off balance,' says Sally, a secretary in a publishing house. If you decide to be unflappable and to learn from the conversation, you will develop another skill: dealing with difficult people. Steve Manton runs a direct marketing consultancy, M Consulting, where staff are often given the brush-off: 'There is nothing more satisfying than dealing with someone who starts off being obnoxious and aggressive and ends up thanking you for your help, understanding and assistance.' One advantage of dealing with someone irate is that you are immediately pitched onto an emotional plane that is usually beyond the bounds of formality. If you can convert that heightened emotion into a positive feeling, you can create a large debt of gratitude.

6 Listen carefully and empathise with someone making a complaint, even if he or she is wrong. You don't have to compromise your company or colleagues if you say things like 'I can see why you were annoyed if you thought we had forgotten about you . . .'. Agree a course of action and stick to it. Many complainants will be satisfied if treated courteously – such as when a senior member of your department explains the situation personally.

7 Accept with grace that the buck will sometimes stop with you – even when you are innocent. Don't tell upset callers that it's not your fault they have been holding the line for 10 minutes. Do the decent thing: cheer them up by apologising.

8 Don't be dragged down by being patronised. People who are condescending to secretaries, for instance, can be shown a quiet dignity. Such callers may not acknowledge it, but they will often get the message. When someone says 'You won't forget that, now,' say, 'No, you can rely on me.'

9 **Try** always to be courteous for your own sake, says Wilks. 'If someone is nice to you on the phone it improves the lot of everybody,' she says. 'But bad emotions, particularly anger and despair, are catching.'

How to write memos

1 **Understand** that a memo is a tool of the expert office politician – crucial in proving one's innocence. When your boss tells you to do something that is likely to rebound – to take dangerous short cuts, for instance – you can write: 'Following our discussion, I thought it useful to make a note of your instructions to me. . .'. This will be helpful evidence in the post-mortem. Remember that the Franks Inquiry (set up to establish who was responsible for the British Government's being caught napping when the Argentinians invaded the Falkland Islands in 1982) focused several times on who had seen which memo.

2 **Think** of other ways of delivering your message. 'Face-to-face communication should always be the preferred starting point,' says Industrial Relations Services in its report *Communication in the Workplace*. It lists one advantage of memos (they are quick to deliver) but four disadvantages: 'Frequently unread . . . may miss targeted audience . . . no opportunity for feedback . . . impersonal.'

3 **Decide** what you want to achieve – to cover your back, to boast, to blame someone else or to provide information.

4 **Make** clear the reason for your memo early on: 'I spoke to Bernie yesterday and thought I should keep you informed . . .' or 'Anthea wants you to execute plan B immediately.' Put technical information in appendices: memos should be short and demonstrate succinct phrasing.

5 **Avoid** releasing your frustrations on paper. Memos are often kept and so can be a permanent witness to your five-minute fury over the state of the rubbish bins. Angry notes will be dwelt on by colleagues – and analysed in detail by subordinates who, perhaps not knowing you well, will be intrigued by any insight into your character. If you are cross with people, it is nearly always better to deal with them directly: there are often mitigating circumstances.

6 **Be** careful with memos intended for wide circulation. Show them to one or two colleagues first. Avoid feeble jokes, but understand that if you are genuinely funny, your memos will be widely and religiously read.

7 **Adopt** a cautious stance in memos about others: some personnel officers may take an authoritarian and suspicious viewpoint. Former diplomat 'Sam' often saw confidential files on colleagues to which senior staff had been asked to add their remarks: 'These memos were always fascinating – but said more about the writer.'

8 **Get** worried if there is a constant flow of buck-passing memos in your company: you operate in a 'blame culture', where colleagues are used to finding scapegoats. Keep copies, with a spare set at home if your workmates seem particularly cynical.

●●●

How to write a report

1 **Work** out why the report is needed. Some organisations (firms of auditors, for instance, and research companies) like to impress their clients with fat files of information. But, increasingly, managers are turning to the 'slim is beautiful' school of thought.

2 **Keep** the report as short as possible if you are writing it for efficient people. One or two pages, with more complex parts relegated to appendices, will be enough for most internal reports. Put in an 'executive summary' and a synopsis of conclusions if the report is much longer.

3 **Make** the report as consistent as possible. Readers will have reason to get restless if your research seems to be pointing in different directions. In the best reports, the underlying inconsistencies are reconciled or prioritised by the author. You do this by saying things like 'Although our previous experiences in Croydon were not positive, we believe that the omens are more favourable now.'

4 **Follow** the current fashion for highlighting action points. In the past, a large report was often regarded as an achievement in itself – particularly by civil servants. Nowadays, few reports are complete without an added sense of momentum. Timetables and schedules give a sense of direction – and are useful in co-ordinating activities and highlighting 'dependency links' where, for instance, the marketing department cannot deliver its part of the agreement until it gets some information from accounts. IT consultant David says: 'Many of the big IT projects that go down the drain do so because people didn't follow up the dependency links.'

5 **Write** up reports as soon as possible. You lose large parts of your recollection even the day after a meeting takes place. People are usually extremely impressed to receive a report in a day or two.

6 **Don't** feel tied by the formal language that used to characterise reports. You probably do not need to refer to people as Mr, for instance. Similarly, although you should usually avoid including jokes, you can still try to make people smile with the odd understated comment or interesting observation. Readers of reports are often appreciative of efforts to vary the tone and keep them interested.

How to get the best out of being on a committee

1 **Decide** what you can offer the committee and what it can offer you. Some meetings are primarily an occasional excuse for a glass of wine and a chat; others make serious decisions.

2 **Know** before each meeting what you want out of it. At the very least, read the paperwork closely beforehand.

3 **Square** your allies on important decisions in advance: co-ordinate your response to likely foes. 'It's all about homework and what happens in the alliances,' says former Civil Servant and committee doyenne Rosa Prentice. 'The committee meeting should be a matter of rubber-stamping.' Preparation is particularly important if you have a weak chair who lets the conversation ramble and frequently gives in to procedural points.

4 **Time** your intervention, suggests consultant Basil Gilbert, another committee veteran: 'If there is a long discussion, don't go first. Fourth or fifth can set the tone for the rest of the debate.'

5 **Give** in, gracefully but conspicuously, on issues you don't really care about. Appearing to put up a fight can be particularly useful if you are preparing for battle on another subject. Always remember the British sense of compromise: you need to give your opponents some victories to cover their losses. If you set the agenda, you may be able to get passions exercised and egos satisfied before reaching items you care about. Colleagues may exhaust themselves discussing the canteen menu – leaving them little energy to challenge the US investment plans.

6 **Threaten** resignation only in the direst of circumstances. Prentice warns: 'Do not make threats that cannot be carried out.'

How to get the best out of meetings

1 Know what you want before the meeting starts. Do you want to put yourself in a good light? Do you want to achieve a certain end?

2 Prepare by reading any papers circulated beforehand, working out your own strategy and sounding out potential allies on crucial issues. It may sound boring, but solid preparation keeps many senior executives alive. Some boardrooms are dominated by uninspiring but meticulous people who survive on their ability to manipulate meetings.

3 Don't expect the most important issues to be given the most time. Accountant Paul Le Druillenec has been attending meetings for 20 years: 'People won't discuss budgets of millions of pounds, because they don't understand them. But keep to the end of the meeting discussions about the colour of the curtains or what kind of wine to serve, because everyone is an expert.'

4 Expect the meeting to be a mess if you don't have an agenda or if more than about 15 people are taking part.

5 Sound positive. Never lose your temper and don't be blunt in your criticisms. Former Civil Servant Teresa Supola says, 'Subtle destruction of someone else's idea by Socratic questioning is a better way of doing things. If someone suggests a terrible idea, you say what a good idea it is and then add: "But may I just ask one question . . . ?"' Don't criticise paragraph 43 of someone else's major *œuvre* without saying something nice first.

6 **Stick** to the points on the agenda. Those who ramble and repeat themselves get a reputation as bores. The old days of meetings lasting 10 hours have largely gone.

7 **Let** other people take the credit for your ideas if your main goal is to get those ideas accepted. Say, for example, 'I would really like to endorse Brendan's earlier suggestion that . . .'. Brendan may have said only half of what you implied that he did, but he may feel so flattered by your words that he barely notices the embellishment.

8 **Listen** and learn. The most adept participants are often not the ones who say the most: they have often set up colleagues beforehand to do some of the work for them. The best practitioners are also accomplished deployers of the strategic red herring, the well-timed departure and other advanced techniques.

9 **Make** sure you keep all the commitments you made in the meeting. You quickly lose Brownie points with colleagues if you fight like a dog on the floor only to forget it all afterwards.

How to chair a meeting

1 **Recognise** that the most important part of the job is showing a sense of direction. You shouldn't dominate the meeting yourself, and may not have strong views on each agenda item, but you must convey a sense of purpose to everyone else. You will be blamed and resented if you lose control and regularly allow discussions to meander.

2 **Familiarise** yourself with each item beforehand. You need to win the respect of all participants – and a mastery of detail, subtly disclosed, is one way to achieve this. Similarly, you will be held in awe if you can summarise debates succinctly and objectively.

3 **Ensure** that all committee members have the papers they need. You demonstrate incompetence if people have to read important documents on the spot. Don't let other people get away with coming unprepared or late.

4 **'Always** ask yourself how the winners and losers on each agenda item will feel afterwards,' says former business consultant and regular chairman Patrick Burton. Find ways to compensate people for losing: they should at least have their say and should perhaps appear to get victories on other agenda points. The psychological dimension is crucial. Some chairs complete meetings in 20 minutes, but leave the participants seething for hours. Ideally, discussions will be satisfying emotionally as well as intellectually.

5 Encourage the shy and muffle the verbose. Remember what Yeats wrote: 'The best lack all conviction, while the worst are full of passionate intensity.' Your task will be eased if you set a pattern of short, sharp interjections that are always focused. It is surprisingly easy to spend an hour discussing a theoretical point that is, in practice, resolved by a minor amendment.

6 Keep a set of formulae for compromises up your sleeve. A good chair needs to be able to reconcile different views. If you are working in a fast-changing environment, it is no weakness to say, 'It's clear from our discussion that we all need to find out more about this area. We need to come back to this next time.'

7 Exude an aura of well-being and good humour. Build up a stock of pleasant phrases to sugar the pill when cutting people off or stopping rows between other committee members. Understand that other people will be jockeying for position, but don't let this branch of office politics undermine the proceedings.

8 Devise follow-up procedures to ensure that all 'action points' are implemented. 'Make sure you are chummy with the person doing the minutes,' says veteran chairwoman Hermione Hayes. 'You need to see them before they go out.' Some points are too delicate and others may need to be 'spin-doctored'.

How to get the best from brainstorming sessions

1 Expect confusion if your company has never run brainstorming sessions before: they are more difficult to organise than people realise. If there are more than five or six participants, it is more likely to become competitive than co-operative.

2 Take your lead from the person running the session. Some companies bring in outside facilitators. Someone performing this role well will explain the parameters and explain that you will not get a black mark on your file if you make outlandish suggestions. If the facilitator does not make these points clear, ask for clarification at the start.

3 Don't expect to come up with creative ideas for more than about 45 minutes, and try not to be drawn into more than one session every two or three weeks. When they work well, brainstorms are emotionally demanding exercises in which you show a more imaginative, wilder side than usual at work. 'They give people the chance to push back the limits of the ordinary,' says business consultant and freelance facilitator Elaine Mercer.

4 Be flattered that you were invited to participate. Many companies will not invite wallflowers. But recognise that brainstorming is better suited to creative activities – coming up with the name of a new product, for example – than to technical occupations.

5 **Follow** up on other people's ideas during the session as well as throwing in your own.

6 **Leave** a gap between the session and implementing ideas. You need a few hours at the very least before the exuberance of a good session has worn off.

7 **Don't** feel that you have failed if you are inhibited by the presence of your bosses and other senior staff. The most productive sessions do not occur when people are apprehensive about one another.

• •

How to make a presentation

1 **Understand** that audiences usually enjoy an atmosphere of certainty. You may think you are giving balance by saying 'On the one hand . . . on the other . . . just possibly . . .', but if you do this too much, you will confuse and worry your listeners. Pollster Bob Worcester of Mori is a great success as a speaker partly because he makes firm predictions.

2 **Give** the impression of some informality. 'Let the audience think they can ask you questions when they want – even if you don't want them to,' says part-time lecturer Bettina Bourne. This leaves them with the reassuring, though false, impression that they are still in control. Always give them a question and answer session at the end. Interaction gives you an opportunity to prove that you are a human being.

3 **Keep** your audience's attention. 'The maximum practical concentration span on any one voice is about 10 or 11 minutes,' says Simon Bruxner-Randall of the Imagination consultancy. 'You can have up to three presenters – but not more, because it then becomes disjointed.'

4 **Remember** that jokes can be as important as the serious bits, but a subtle touch is usually more appropriate than belly-laughs. Don't try to adopt a persona that isn't your own, and never make jokes you are uncomfortable with: your audience will get embarrassed.

5 **Always** have a fall-back plan. If you do presentations regularly, it is only a matter of time before you are let down by technology. Don't depend completely on other people. Hotel staff will often promise you a particular room or a television set and then change the arrangements at the last minute.

6 **Practise** your presentation in front of a friendly audience first. If you know your subject well, you will probably use jargon or phrases that others don't understand. Some presenters speak too quickly, and many use difficult vocabulary in the mistaken belief that it will impress. People who like gadgets will sometimes make too much use of technology.

7 **Avoid** giving handouts at the start of your talk. At least half your audience will read them rather than listen to you. If you want to leave them a handout at the end, give something extra, not just a reproduction of your slides.

Vary your presentations. If you get bored with what you say, you can be sure your listeners will too. Insurance salespeople are very practised presenters, but often appear insincere because they say the same things to everyone. Be careful about using tailor-made presentation software: people used to seeing presentations can tell very quickly whether you have followed the standard programs.

How to behave at conferences

Recognise the limitations of the conference scene – a gravy train for many organisers, who can charge more than £500 a day to delegates.

Decide why you are going – to get contacts, information or a break from the office. 'The speakers are often the least important part,' says consultant Sean Blythe. Many give the same presentation each time.

Think of an interesting way to introduce yourself. 'I was intrigued by the point you made about Boris Karloff' is more interesting than 'May I join you?'

Sit near the door during long speeches. Conference organisers give exotic titles to dull subjects. Take notes if you are having difficulty staying awake.

Follow the 'ABC' rule if you ask a question: Always Be Cheerful. Even if your question is a difficult one, you can usually find a way of putting it politely. Asking a question is a useful way of signposting your presence. If you ask a good one, people will be impressed. If you ask 14, they will get restless. Listen carefully to the responses. 'It's when they answer questions that speakers often start talking naturally,' says PR consultant Alison Sutherland.

6 Watch practised conference-goers. Dave Dobbs is on the medical circuit: 'You need to rush round the exhibitors to get as many freebies as possible. Target the people giving away umbrellas and cakes – because there won't be any left by the first lunchtime.'

7 Consider your attitude to temptation. Residential courses, particularly those at weekends, are sometimes described as 'Club 40-60'. Organisers often soak speakers and delegates in alcohol as a way of dampening down complaints about the programme.

8 Decide how you will report back to your colleagues and bosses. The speakers and participants list could be useful to your marketing department. The fact that competitor companies were there (or not there) could be a reason for going to the next one. If you are really keen to go back, you can write a report and make action points. Even the most tangential of recommendations can make you look dynamic and purposeful.

How to get the best out of a business lunch

1 **Recognise** that the long, boozy lunches of the 1980s have changed guise. If you still have time for many of these jaunts, you are out of date. Even bon vivants now take a puritanical view. There are now two categories of lunch: the shorter, sharper meeting at which information is transmitted, and the long day out including lunch during which little information is exchanged but the two parties are supposed to bond. Completely different rules apply to each occasion.

2 **Accept** that the lean, mean lunch can still be invaluable in the right circumstances. If you need to pick someone's brain, the job can be enlivened by food. Journalists often get their best stories in the restaurant – at the stage by which the main subjects have been covered and the diners are searching for new topics. People in creative roles often stimulate their minds by getting away from the desk. And lunches are particularly useful for exchanging indiscretions.

3 **Understand** that many people will see an invitation as a bribe. The Corporate Hospitality and Events Association believes that it is usually far better to invite suppliers, rather than potential clients to days out and lunches at Ascot, Wimbledon and other venues. 'You are trying to build a better relationship with suppliers,' says spokesman Wayne Moss. 'If you invite a customer, they think you are going to ask them to raise the order size.'

Bonding events – where people drive tanks or aircraft, for example – are becoming increasingly popular with both male and female guests. 'Intimate discussions are seen to be a thing of the past,' says Moss. 'In many cases, you are just building the relationship and not talking about work at all.'

4 Decide what you want from the exchange – which points should be discussed (or ignored) and what action you want to take afterwards. Journalist Maria Scott says, 'It is nearly always worthwhile investing time in preparation. Five minutes thinking about the issues facing the other person's employer often pays large dividends.' And even the most cynical types are flattered if you show an understanding of their role: 'I saw your hallmarks on the design of the new pension plan . . .'.

5 Resist the line, much favoured by older men at shorter lunches, of 'So, what are your hobbies?' Far from putting people at their ease, this clumsy question will be irksome to people who are efficient and busy. They know that you have no genuine interest in their private life and would much rather keep talking about fidelity insurance or whatever subject it was that you met to discuss.

6 Consider the alternatives. David Evans, a PR consultant, had long lunches during the 1980s but now meets contacts for a drink after work: 'There is a lot of time pressure now – and a lunch can take the best part of three hours.' The rise of the wine bar is also encouraging the rise in quick, informal lunches.

Understanding the characters

•••

How to deal with a bureaucrat

1 **Understand** the usual demeanour of bureaucrats: 'generally pleasant and mild-mannered but . . . often excessively slow and cautious in making decisions', according to psychologists Cary Cooper and Susan Cartwright in their book *Managing Workplace Stress*. They are in their jobs for the pensions and are unlikely to change just for you.

2 **Avoid** confrontation and don't get angry when they say, 'Well, we've never done it that way before and I've been here since 1973.' Whacky, creative ideas will rarely succeed with employees whose lives and promotion prospects depend on their conformity. 'You just go by the rules all the time,' says Gary, a former Customs and Excise officer, 'and not according to any extenuating circumstances. People with extenuating circumstances get totally frustrated.'

3 **Recognise** that *you* have to know the rules better than *they* do to win. The most dedicated will even help you break the rules, by inventing such ruses as new precedents or interpretations, a favourite technique of the Civil Servants in the television series *Yes Minister*. 'Conspiratorial flattery is very useful,' says Maria, a former Department of Trade and Industry high-flier. 'A lot of bureaucrats are dying to break out. But it's fear that stops them.'

4 **Rarely** rely on them to argue your case with others or try to get you a fair settlement. Senior ones will sometimes be helpful, but their juniors are often blinkered. A major reason that millions of people lose out on state benefits is that frontline social security staff do not understand the whole system and are often encouraged to cut claims rather than get people their full entitlement.

5 **Ask** for the name of the bureaucrat's boss, suggests Gary. 'Nothing struck such fear into me as that. If someone got an MP to write a letter for them, the whole office would stop.'

How to deal with a procrastinator

1 **Recognise** that this type of person can cause damage without realising it. Not returning phone calls or postponing decisions to invest in new technology are greater sins than they might seem. Staff become demoralised if their efforts are blocked for no good reason.

Find out why they delay. Some people procrastinate about everything, and most of us put off doing some things. Employees who are very circumspect are a liability in a fast-changing environment, but could be a boon if they work in security, accountancy or a field where caution is valued.

Decide on a plan of campaign if the procrastinators are causing damage. 'Sometimes it's a case of giving a firm kick, sometimes it's better to lead by persuasion,' says former Civil Servant Patrick Larkin. A creative procrastinator may respond well to someone else doing the administration he loathes. It is more difficult to rearrange working operations if the procrastinator is in charge of you, but now that companies are becoming more flexible you can probably find opportunities to initiate change, if you are subtle. Someone who doesn't open mail, for example, could have it done for them.

Cover all avenues if you are dealing with a strategic procrastinator. This sort of person will postpone signing a major deal unless all the details have been double-checked. 'Have the answers to all questions: you mustn't give them opportunities through sloppiness,' says Larkin.

Be careful not to send a procrastinator into a panic by barking at the wrong moment. Michael Carroll of consultancy Right Cavendish says, 'Unless you help them, you create more stress and don't solve the problem.' Those who need to stay up all night to finish a report that they have delayed are emotionally vulnerable and could even down tools if you show your frustration.

How to deal with a visionary

1 **Remember** that although visionaries may love mankind in general, they are not always so keen on the individual flesh-and-blood specimens. Just because they are trying to save the world doesn't mean they will be nice to you.

2 **Observe** closely to see whether you can work with them at all. 'If the person is a megalomaniac visionary, like Robert Maxwell, don't touch them,' says Una Maguire, a former teacher who became an expert in workplace politics. 'But if you are talking about someone mystical, imaginative, daft and unable to remember what they did yesterday, it can be wonderful.' Some visionaries – Richard Branson, for example – are susceptible to logic but others – such as Baroness Thatcher and Dame Barbara Cartland – are said to become more immune to human influence the more elevated they become.

3 **Get** them to be specific about their vision. Get it in writing if you can. The one thing worse than dying for a cause is dying for a cause you do not believe in. Few visionaries will admit that their vision is faulty: they are more likely to say you did a bad job of implementing it.

4 **Avoid** confrontation with the most extreme visionaries: it can only end badly. True visionaries will die for their beliefs or, at the very least, sacrifice you.

5 **Learn** from charismatic and inspiring people. Florence Nightingale may have been widely regarded as difficult, but she filled her supporters with purpose.

6 **Steer** clear of inept visionaries. Zest and clumsiness make a disastrous combination. As well as being ruined, you will look ridiculous.

• •
How to deal with a prima donna

1 **Find** out if you are dealing with a true prima donna by trying to make a human connection. Appeal to their better nature, ask them to see things from another perspective. The genuine articles will find it difficult to understand you. They are usually poor at adult relationships: like Scarlett O'Hara in *Gone with the Wind*, they prefer nanny figures and slaves. You can probably reach rational conclusions with people who are merely overemotional, even though you have to work hard to get there.

2 **Accept** that some prima donnas cannot work any other way. Either you part company or you put up with them. 'We have to recognise that certain people are outstandingly brilliant,' says psychotherapist Frances Wilks, who runs self-development courses for the City University, London. 'As long as they deliver the goods there is a kind of contract going on. Marilyn Monroe annoyed everyone she worked with, but she was brilliant.'

3 **Limit** their potential for damage. 'Create a cocoon around them where they can still work but be managed and contained,' suggests occupational psychologist Michael Carroll of consultancy Right Cavendish. In this way they can arrive late, work through the night, have tantrums and weep without upsetting everyone else.

4 **Be** firm but kind in resisting unreasonable demands. 'Once any narcissistic person knows they can break the rules, they run all over you,' says Carroll. Don't immediately move your 8.00 am meeting to 10.30 just because they can't concentrate in the early morning. But be ready to give prima donnas the reassurance and recognition they crave. Expect explosions, sulking, depression and theatricals if you criticise them. These are the sort of people who will imagine you looking remorseful at their funeral.

5 **Don't** let yourself feel second-rate. 'Dealing with a prima donna does involve us in being very clear about our own worth,' says Wilks. 'You have to recognise their genius without feeling envious.'

6 **Understand** that they tend to work in certain environments – particularly politics, the media and the arts. They rarely get promoted in business because they usually lack organisational and managerial abilities. On the rare occasions when they get to the top because of their flair, the results are usually catastrophic. Get rid of them quickly if they are damaging the organisation. But, handled with firmness and reassurance, prima donnas can have a wonderful career.

How to deal with a perfectionist

1 **Recognise** that there are two categories: the traditional perfectionist and slavemaster who demands 100 per cent of himself and others all the time; and the long-term player who learns from mistakes and accepts 80 or 90 per cent achievement as the maximum obtainable day to day. The traditional perfectionist is never easy to deal with. People in the second category are not true perfectionists, in that they often relish turning errors to their advantage, but they get closer to excellence over the long haul.

2 **Expect** genuine perfectionists to create chaos. They are usually poor at prioritising and working to deadlines. They perform particularly badly if left to their own devices on creative long-term projects. Accountant and business adviser Paul Le Druillenec says, 'They have to be checked at least twice an hour – and, if you are lucky, you will get good-quality work from them. But if you ask a perfectionist to design an invoice for you and let them go unchecked, they will still be selecting the right shades and fonts three weeks later.' They are the kind of people who produce marvellous competition entries two weeks after the closing date. The exquisite chef in the Stanley Tucci film *Big Night* refused to pander to the low tastes of his clientele and quickly and painfully lost his restaurant.

3 **Attempt** to reason with them, but and avoid getting into shouting matches, advises psychotherapist Frances

Wilks of City University: 'They have an inner voice telling them to be perfect. They are reflecting their own fears when they tell you to be perfect. If you shout at them, you'll make the parent in them feel they were justified.'

Spot them quickly and avoid working with them. Behavioural hallmarks include perfectionist dressing (razor creases in jeans, spotless shoes), strange personal preferences (ironed bedsheets), few friends at work, and a combination of disappointment and striving for the best. They often dislike change, says Wilks: 'Perfectionism is about rigidity: if you want things perfect, you want them in a steady state. It destroys relationships.'

Avoid putting perfectionists in control of others. They are usually bad team players. Some of the most attractive characters give the (misleading) impression of being at the other end of the spectrum – for example, leading politicians Mo Mowlam, who has taken off her wig in meetings with journalists, and former Chancellor Kenneth Clarke, who made famous the combination of brown suede shoes and dark suits. 'Working for perfectionists is hell,' says researcher Nanette Ryan. 'But they will be the same to everyone – and eventually there will be a revolt.'

• •

How to deal with an autocrat

Work out which type you are dealing with – the high-flier (James Goldsmith, Sam Goldwyn) or the small-time Stalin. Although they share a thirst for power, the two types of autocrat are polarised between those whose vision propels them to success and those who spend their lives fighting over important-looking chairs. In between there are others who are so effective and decisive that they can *seem* like dictators to quieter colleagues. Anyone with a sense of humour is unlikely to be a genuine autocrat.

Avoid confrontation – unless you are going in for the kill. Only a few people were quicker in the ring than Margaret Thatcher or Robert Maxwell. 'In extreme cases, autocrats are often brought down by a grouping of subordinates,' say Cary Cooper and Susan Cartwright in their book, *Managing Workplace Stress*.

Realise that ingratiation is a way of life for many who love power. They go cap in hand to those above them but enjoy it if you tug your forelock to them. This can make for undemanding bosses, says part-time lecturer Tom Gamble: 'They are so busy firing off instructions, they can't remember who or what they asked. When they say they are going to rebuild Hadrian's Wall, you have to say, "Yes, of course, sir. We'll start ordering the bricks tomorrow." But you won't even have to look up from your desk because they will soon forget they asked.' Beware, though, that some autocrats make mental notes of all their conversations.

Cultivate any sources of power that could also give you a lever against the autocrats: for example, a source of information they lack – (eg you play tennis with the company's best customer or simply understand the computer systems). Keep memos and contemporaneous notes if you believe you are heading for trouble.

5 Watch out for the toadies, warns psychotherapist and City University personal development course director Frances Wilks. 'Autocrats can attract people who are quite weak. These toadies are dangerous people who will report back on you and fight the autocrat's corner for them.'

6 Stick with brilliant autocrats. Hundreds of people can rise on the back of one innovator. 'It's probably good to work for someone like Thatcher,' says Gamble. 'But don't spend your life doing it.'

7 Understand that some autocrats retain a court jester to suggest they have a softer side. But don't take this as a cue to copy the role. Prime Minister Tony Blair may have done this when he made Tony Banks his sports minister, but other ministers have refrained from demonstrating such an exuberance of humour and independent-mindedness.

. . . .
How to deal with someone who panics

1 Understand that nearly everyone will panic under the right circumstances: when it happens, you lose your ability to filter information, to prioritise and to react sensibly to events. Panic, where you are overwhelmed with fear can, however, be contained by soldiers, police officers and others who can discipline emotions. 'Policemen can deal wonderfully with a terrible situation and then have nightmares afterwards,' says Michael Carroll of consultancy Right Cavendish. 'People who go through a major conflict like a war often feel the effects afterwards. Post-traumatic stress disorder is a form of panic.'

2 Distinguish between acute and chronic panickers. Someone suffering an acute panic attack probably needs kind words, reassurance, a cup of tea and privacy. 'It's the equivalent of talking to a horse,' says John, a regular sufferer. 'Keep saying reassuring things: it doesn't really matter what they are. "You're OK, don't worry" and so on.' Dizziness, stomach churning and other symptoms are likely to be reduced if the sufferer takes in more oxygen by breathing deeply a few times.

3 Recognise the signs of chronic panic: people who are unable to meet deadlines, drop assignments without notice and get angry under pressure. Common causes are low self-esteem, perfectionism and poor time management. 'Reassure them that what you are expecting is not the be-all and end-all,' says psychotherapist Frances Wilks of City University. 'But at the same time you need to keep the pressure going. Give them a tighter deadline than you need but don't tell them that.' Avoid shouting at them: as well as frightening them even more, it implies that they are right to panic.

4 Help people prepare for frightening situations. People appearing on radio or television are less likely to panic if they have practised in a studio beforehand, says public relations consultant Michelle Lloyd-Jones. Occupational psychologist Sandi Mann of Salford University advocates the 'What is the worst that could happen?' approach for people frightened of making presentations or giving speeches. 'A common fear is "What happens if I'm asked a question I can't answer?" or "What happens if I fall over on stage?" You can plan for these possibilities in advance – even write them down. You can say, "That's an excellent question; I don't know the answer but I'll research it when I get back to my office." If you fall over, you can make a joke to the audience ("I think I'm falling for you already") and it can come over as very human.'

5 **Ensure** that the panic does not spread to other people. When Corporal Jones panics in television's *Dad's Army* the others recognise the symptoms immediately (he starts shouting 'Don't panic!') and firmly tell him to stop.

Parties and other events

How to behave at a party

1 Don't automatically let your hair down. There are parties and parties. Soldiers on the eve of battle – like the submariners in the film *Das Boot* – can afford to be carried out the door, but employers are usually less tolerant of inebriation these days. Companies increasingly host gatherings to impress their clients, in which case your have to be on best behaviour. You may have to pretend to be relaxed – or a bit 'giggly' if you are female – but you should recognise that you are not there to enjoy yourself. Parties can be deadly serious: the main character in the 1998 film *Sliding Doors* lost her job as a consequence of an informal party.

2 Take your cue from the bosses. If senior ranks are represented in large numbers and not drinking, a certain level of decorum is required. Managers usually recognise, however, that the occasion is a good opportunity for you to ask them 'frank questions'. Employment lawyer Paul Nicholls regularly throws parties for his staff in the Manchester office of Dibb Lupton Alsop: 'You can't overestimate the importance of a good party. After a couple of glasses, people have the courage to confront you with what is troubling them. It can be a bit painful but it's much better than not hearing it.'

3 **Accept** that the main reason for the event is for people to meet one another. Try not to spend the evening with the people you know best in your department. Most people are surprisingly shy, when sober. You can become a big hit just by chatting to one or two others who then introduce you to their colleagues.

4 **Give** yourself a job if you are feeling at a loose end. Handing crisps round and showing people where to hang their coats is a fruitful way of making that first awkward contact. If you share a joke, however feeble ('Nice coat – I think I'll take that one later'), you have started a theme that you can return to ('Now where did you get that mac? Hard to get good waterproofs these days.').

5 **Introduce** yourself to other people confidently, if all else fails and you are left alone. If you have a welcome for yourself and a smile, others usually follow suit. Shake hands if it is a formal occasion, and get others interested by asking them about themselves ('Why is it you accounts people are so busy these days?').

6 **Treat** others well and you'll get the same back. Encourage people to join your group who are standing alone. Introduce people to each other, even if connections are tenuous ('Meet Sam – another Abba fan'). Never leave someone on their own – a gawky, ill-assured act of rejection. Introduce them to a colleague instead.

7 **Don't** be cast in gloom if you overdid it. Excessive alcohol makes drinkers feel guilty anyway. The chances are that few people noticed – and others will like you for showing an unexpected bit of spirit. If things were really bad, you might need to make apologies, but most people are disarmed by an honest acceptance of fallibility.

How to organise a party

1 **Don't** give control to just one person – even if it's you. Administrator Roger's teetotal and totalitarian boss organises all the Christmas parties. In 1995 the department sang hymns accompanied by an accordionist; in 1996 they were given celery and sliced mushrooms in tomato ketchup dip; the next year they were told their guests would be vetted. You are better off setting up a small committee to decide the time, venue and other arrangements. This way, you are also less likely to be blamed when people say it was no good – and someone usually does.

2 **Avoid** serving drink without food, warns employment solicitor James Davies of solicitors Lewis Silkin. Employers can face unlimited damages for sexual harassment and can be held liable for property damage or personal injury. 'Every January we get phone calls because claims and problems have arisen from Christmas parties', he says. He advises employers to tell staff beforehand 'that they should behave in an appropriate manner to colleagues and watch how much alcohol they consume'. Making advances to colleagues can result in a claim if they object. Curtis Hanson's film *LA Confidential* hinges on a drunken and violent Christmas party.

3 **Make** sure the company is seen to be generous. It should build the cost of the party into its budget, according to consultant Robin Linnecar of the Change Partnership: 'Something as simple as a party can show everyone is dependent on everyone else. Employers need to reinforce that point.'

4 **Remember** the practical points. Staff will feel depressed if you book a room that looks empty even when you are all there – especially if there is a wild party next door. Don't leave a gap between the end of the working day and the start of the party. Avoid forcing staff to travel long distances (unless you are paying fares there and back) or to spend money hiring suits. Don't announce any cutbacks, and keep any speeches short.

5 **Don't** believe your staff will trust you when you metamorphose from office dictator to good-time guy for the party. They will probably laugh at your jokes and dance with you if you ask but might be grimacing behind your back. 'We used to have to indulge the partners,' says Maurice of his accountancy firm days. 'The idea was supposed to be "Oh, Eric's just a normal human being even though he's on £200,000."'

6 **Go** early if you are the boss, unless you are a party animal and popular. 'If your superiors don't come at all, that is seen as bad,' says Roger. 'Ideally, they should come early when everyone is sober and can remember they were there. They should hang around an hour or so and then go, so that they aren't inhibiting people who want to get drunk and slag off everyone.'

7 **Expect** a dip in productivity the next day. Unless you have specifically told people to be on time, you should turn a blind eye if some are late. Davies says, 'To some extent, employers are unreasonable to complain if they have laid on limitless free drink.'

How to deal with a hangover

1 **Keep** a low profile at work and try to pretend that you don't have a hangover. Bosses are becoming increasingly puritanical about drink – even those, paradoxically, who encourage staff to 'Work hard, play hard.' 'It's a major taboo,' says Jo Bond of Coutts Career Consulting. 'It's not acceptable behaviour if you look sick and disappear to throw up.' If your bosses want to put you on the down-sizing list, they will seize on persistent hangovers as a justification. Frank, who once drank eight pints a night, now saves himself for the weekends, but works hard at covering up a weekday lapse: 'You've got to remember that people have good days and bad days for all sorts of reasons. If you drink a lot of mouthwash and are pretty much working on your own, you should be OK.'

2 Give the impression that your overindulgence is unlikely to recur – if you feel forced into making any mention of it at all. Lydia is a regular drinker but, on the rare occasions that colleagues have suspected a hangover, has suggested that she was celebrating her wedding anniversary or another special event: 'You don't want people thinking that it's your fourth time this week or that you do it every Thursday.'

3 Don't give the game away by consuming large quantities of water in front of your colleagues. Avoid long discussions. Other people might notice that you are not your usual self. You are also likely to be feeling irritable. People who are usually sunny-natured might find they are more capable of making complaints or tackling difficult colleagues.

4 Understand that attitudes vary considerably between different companies and locations. Behaviour that would get a nurse into trouble is *de rigueur* for a rock star. People working in pubs, doctors, sailors and lawyers are the most alcohol-dependent, according to government statistics. But the older you are, the more inappropriate a hangover. Each employee takes an average of half-a-day's sick leave a year because of alcohol-induced illness, according to the Health Education Authority (HEA). Drinkers in the Midlands and East Anglia are less likely to have been drunk in the previous year than people in the rest of England, says the HEA.

5 Avoid telling white lies if by doing so you might put your job in jeopardy. For instance, if you were seen being helped out of the pub one night, don't feel tempted to say you have a bad foot the next day. Solicitor James Davies of Lewis Silkin says: 'Someone is unlikely to be sacked for being late one day or not being at their best because of a hangover. But you can be sacked for being dishonest.' The fact that a hangover is self-induced is not necessarily significant. 'It's no different in this way to someone who strains their back playing squash or skiing,' says Davies.

Don't be surprised at a lack of sympathy from peers. Writing in the *British Medical Journal*, hangover specialist Dr Ian Calder says, 'Psychosocial factors such as guilt about drinking, a neurotic personality, becoming angry or depressed while drinking, and having suffered 'negative life events' in the previous 12 months are better predictors of hangover symptoms than the amount of ethanol drunk.'

• •

How to survive April Fool's Day

Put yourself on emergency stations if you are deeply pompous: you are exactly the kind of person other people will be queuing up to avenge themselves on.

Keep alert all day. Question in your mind all unusual requests. Even the most eminent have returned bogus calls to Mr L E Fant at London Zoo – to the delight of colleagues.

Do your best to laugh uproariously when you dis-cover that you have been glued to your chair by your workmates. If you get furious the tale will live forever, and will be told in exaggerated detail to everyone who comes into your department. If you smile you may at least get the reputation of being a good sport – and you can then start plotting your revenge for next year.

Consider whether you should get in there first. But remember that it is a rare boss who likes being cut down to size in public. Make sure you clean your fingerprints off the whoopee cushion first.

Learn from the experts in the field: the teachers who each year dodge water buckets balanced on doors and a variety of other booby traps. Retired teacher Margot Pelz usually managed to outwit the children throughout her career in the classroom: 'On the whole, the teachers were in advance of the kids and tended to do something first. We might say they had a three-hour test or that they were going on a field trip when it was pouring with rain.'

Sickness and stress

....
How to ring in sick

1 **Understand** that people who take 'sickies' can be disciplined or lose their job if found out. Employees seen at the races while suffering from 'flu are probably guilty of gross misconduct and may be instantly dismissed. 'It's utter dishonesty and a complete breach of good faith,' says employment solicitor Michael Burd of Lewis Silkin.

2 **Call** in as early as possible. Your contract or staff handbook has to contain details about sickness absence. It could say that you need to phone in by a particular time.

3 **Speak** to your boss directly. 'Skivers often deliberately arrange to speak to someone else to avoid being given the third degree,' says accountant Paul Le Druillenec. Messages can be poorly relayed by disbelieving colleagues. Your boss might be told 'Nancy rang in – but she sounded fine to me.' Give a realistic assessment of when you are likely to return: you will cause much irritation if the date is postponed.

4 **Sound** miserable and don't return to the office with a tan. 'Convey the impression that you are sorry you are not there,' says occupational psychologist Sandi Mann of Salford University. 'Your boss won't be happy if you sound as if you are going on holiday.' Sound dispirited even if your symptoms are painless and your favourite film is on TV.

5 **Avoid** being vague about your indisposition. People with genuine back pain can be treated with suspicion because it is commonly cited by malingerers. Self-inflicted problems such as hangovers are an obvious exception, however. They may be described as a serious stomach upset or headache. You won't usually breach your contract by taking time off for a hangover – unless it becomes a regular occurrence.

6 **Visit** the doctor if you are off for a few days. To qualify for Statutory Sick Pay, you need a certificate after seven consecutive days' illness. If your employer urges you to go sooner, the doctor may not comply. 'The doctor is under no obligation to give one sooner,' says a spokeswoman for the British Medical Association. The company may have to pay for a certificate (typically £7.50 at 1997 prices) if it wants one earlier, but this should be spelt out in the employment contract.

7 **Accept** that short, frequent absences will be held against you. 'Avoid taking off Mondays or Fridays or just before a Bank Holiday,' says Jo Bond of Coutts Career Consultants. 'Many companies track Monday and Friday sicknesses to see if there is a pattern emerging.' Some employers now phone people at home to check they are there. Managers are increasingly being asked to debrief staff who are off for just one day. If you believe that you are under suspicion, you could point to your good record or the fact that you offered to do some work from home.

• •

How to cope if you are frequently ill

1 Telephone your employer promptly when you are unable to go to work. People who ring in at 11.00 am lose Brownie points with their bosses just when they need them most.

2 Recognise that you are in a worse position if you suffer a series of different illnesses. Employers and industrial tribunals will be more inclined to view you as a malingerer.

3 Understand that you can legitimately be fired for being unable to do your job. Employers increasingly use absence as a selection criterion for redundancy, but are obliged to treat those with chronic illnesses fairly – for example, to see whether they can find them another job that suits them better. The new Disability Discrimination Act puts those suffering illnesses from backache to depression in a far stronger position. 'There could be 3,000 claims in the first year,' says Michael Burd of solicitors Lewis Silkin. 'Most employers don't know what is about to hit them.'

4 **'Approach** your employers before they approach you,' says Jo Bond of Coutts Career Consultants. Showing that you are prepared to co-operate could make the difference between losing and keeping your job. Your company's doctor may provide a second opinion. You might reach a compromise, say, by working from home sometimes.

5 **Study** the terms of any health insurance policies that you or your company may have bought. Lewis Silkin has seen cases where a company has terminated the employment, only to find that the policy pays out to people who remain employees.

6 **Find** out, if you are a member of your company's pension scheme, whether you are eligible for an ill-health pension.

How to diagnose sick-building syndrome

1 **Understand** that this syndrome is becoming more difficult to diagnose, even though the World Health Organisation says it may affect up to 30 per cent of buildings. Staff may cover up health symptoms because they are too insecure (fearing redundancy, for example) to risk going sick. But if people in your office suffer headaches, lethargy, poor concentration, runny noses and itching, there is a good chance that the cause is in the building, the work environment or in the way jobs are organised.

2 **Recognise** that although the most common site for SBS is a large office building, it can affect most parts of the workforce. Cases have occurred in hospitals and even in the home. Causes are either physical – the ventilation system, poor cleaning or a badly laid-out work station – or to do with the job itself. The Health and Safety Executive says, 'Workers most commonly reporting symptoms tend to have little control over their working environment.'

3 **Break** up routine procedures by taking rest periods and rotating tasks. Job design is one of the most important causes. Good employers consult staff regularly about it.

4 **Resist** the temptation to provide your own technical remedies, says the Building Research Establishment. 'People can think the air is too dry because they are suffering from an irritation in the eye,' says specialist Gary Raw. 'But this is very rare.' Working away from natural air, light and earth can be dehumanising. 'People can shrivel when cut off from these,' says psychotherapist Frances Wilks of City University.

5 **Report** your concerns. Some employers will be slow to respond because the costs of putting things right can be enormous. But put together a case, including such arguments as productivity lost through the problem. Get the support of your union and approach a senior manager – preferably someone you believe will be sympathetic.

6 **Remember** that you have the backing of the law. Employers can be guilty of unfair dismissal if they sack you for staying away from work through genuine fear of catching or exacerbating an illness.

● ●

How to tell if you are overdoing it

1 **Don't** automatically take as a bad omen the fact that you work long hours. Some people love their jobs and don't regard work as a chore. And, occasionally, you need to work too hard. But remember the adage that few people on their deathbeds wish they had spent more time in the office.

2 **It's** a bad sign if, when your friends ask you how you are, you usually talk about work.

3 **When** you go on holiday you feel ill at ease. This usually means that you don't know how to relax.

4 **Relationships** with friends, family and loved ones start to suffer because of the amount of work you do.

5 **You** are concerned that you're not up to the demands made on you and find it difficult to make decisions. Robin Linnecar of the Change Partnership believes that although the signs of overwork may be obvious to everyone else, you may not be aware of what is happening: 'You may only realise when someone else points out that you are as white as a sheet or are looking dishevelled.'

6 **Feelings** of extreme anxiety underlie your working life. You may be particularly concerned about losing your job.

7 **Sleep** patterns are disrupted.

8 **You** lose your creative flair and sense of humour, and start to feel isolated from colleagues.

• •

How to recover from burn-out

1 **Diagnose** your condition. Burn-out is most often the result of working too hard and failing to prioritise, but it also happens for such other reasons as poor workplace relationships. It has three common features: emotional exhaustion, depersonalisation (seeing other people as numbers or objects) and a lack of satisfaction in your achievements. Common symptoms include irritability, aggression, poor organisation, low concentration and loss of a sense of humour – grumpy bosses are often suffering chronic burn-out.

2 **Deal** with the problem before it takes control. Don't ignore physical symptoms. Psychologist Sandi Mann of the BNFL corporate communications unit at Salford University says, 'People start to get minor illnesses such as a cold, but they can't shake it off and it keeps recurring. Eventually it gets so bad they can't get out of bed. The body forces them to take two or three weeks off – whereas if they had looked after themselves it could have been sorted out quickly.' It is far better to tell your boss you need help within the next week or two than to faint on his or her desk.

3 Learn how to prioritise. Although most burn-out cases occur among people in positions of authority and responsibility, there is a high incidence of poor planning. 'You have to accept that your in-tray will always be full,' says Cary Cooper. 'If you have a pile of papers, don't just go through it. You need to rearrange it into four piles which need to be dealt with immediately, in a couple of days, and so on.'

4 Make sure that your working life does not spill into your private life. Those who consistently work long hours burn out quicker than the rest. If you are regularly choosing to work more than 40 hours a week for other than financial reasons, you are probably suffering some kind of job insecurity or low self-esteem.

5 Take part in the simple things in life again: exercise, cooking, watching TV, seeing your family. Those too impatient to queue in a supermarket may tell themselves they are easily bored, but they are more likely to be suffering from unacknowledged stress. Many people suffering burn-out eat and sleep badly. Taking exercise can bring rapid improvements.

6 Talk to a 'natural counsellor' – a friendly colleague who will tell you the truth about yourself. This is particularly important if you have poor working relationships. If you are burning out, you will be intense and unable to put this kind of problem in context. But be careful about speaking to bosses or Personnel: some will be surprisingly sympathetic, but the backwoodspeople will become alarmed.

7 **Take** control of the situation. 'It doesn't solve the problem to say it's the government's fault, your employer's fault, and that it's a rotten world,' says Cooper. If you think the problem through, you might decide to get a new boss, a new job or some more training to make you feel more marketable. The reason that so many teachers are taking early retirement is probably linked to the major changes that have taken place since they began the job.

• •
How to avoid being overworked

1 **Analyse** the causes. Are you trying to impress someone, or is your company badly managed? Apart from occasional crises, you should not be feeling overworked. But job insecurity makes many people accept longer hours.

2 **Learn** to say no. People who overwork subordinates are often thick-skinned and do not respond to subtlety. Businesses that people charge by the hour – bordellos and professional firms, for instance – often have a culture of working 14 hours a day when this is not in fact necessary.

3 **Make** sure people know how hard you are working. Women often try too hard to please and are poor at getting recognition. Compare your output to that of your peers. You may be pleasantly surprised.

4 **Copy** others. The most productive workers rarely put in the longest hours. There is a growing belief among management gurus that many of the most effective employees leave their desks at 5.00 or 5.30 pm.

5 **Talk** to your bosses if you are being overworked. If you can come up with good ideas for reorganisation, they should appreciate that.

6 **Review** your own practices. 'Prioritise,' says consultant Robin Linnecar. 'If you are overworked, you get tired and you compound mistakes you would otherwise not have made.' Sixty per cent of managers cannot meet their deadlines, according to the Institute of Personnel and Development.

Discipline

How to respond if you get a warning letter

1 **Work** out for yourself whether it is justified. Many warnings can be taken at face value as a signal to improve your performance, but some bosses also use this route to vent their spleen or to get rid of people regarded as undesirables.

2 **Set** the record straight in writing if you think the allegations are incorrect. If you do not give your version, your case will be considerably weakened.

3 **Read** your company's disciplinary procedures. If you believe you have been falsely accused, you may be able to appeal. If you believe your employer really is trying to dismiss you, then at least you know what is in store.

4 **Make** an effort to improve your performance if you want to keep your job. If you believe your boss's complaints are justified, you may benefit by showing a willingness to co-operate. You could say that you welcome the opportunity to air these difficult issues and ask the boss to show you how the job could be done well, not just adequately.

Speak to your trade union if you have one. Union reps can tell you how your employer compares with others and how staff have been treated in the past. Experienced union reps can usually tell quickly whether you have stepped out of line or are being victimised.

Don't panic. Some bosses are bad at their jobs and enjoy giving the odd warning to keep staff on their toes. It may be upsetting for you, but nothing further may come of it.

How to act if you face disciplinary proceedings

Look out for warning signals. You are either annoying your bosses or being stitched up. Companies wanting to reduce costs sometimes fire employees on slim grounds. The usual pattern in genuine cases has been that the employee gets away with murder for years until the boss finally snaps. In the late 1990s, however, employers are taking action earlier, though often in a disguised, politically correct fashion. If you are asked to go to counselling for your drink problem, recognise that a disciplinary hearing could be the next step.

2 Read up on the company's disciplinary procedure. Most good employers will attach them to your contract. You will get invaluable information here – for instance, whether you can be accompanied to hearings and whether you get a written list of allegations beforehand. Thousands of companies breach their own rules each year (perhaps when the boss loses his temper and sacks someone on the spot). Industrial tribunals often find in favour of the employee on these technicalities. So, if you see they are forgetting a step you may want to keep that information to yourself.

3 Make notes, start keeping a diary and store useful documents at home. You should build up as much objective information as possible if you are defending the allegations. Get someone impartial to focus on your case – a union rep will be particularly useful. Don't project your frustrations onto the disciplinary panel, warns employment specialist Michael Burd of solicitors Lewis Silkin: 'These are very stressful situations, but you need to keep a cool head. Don't give the panel ammunition to shoot you by letting yourself be provoked.'

4 Consider confessing, if you think your behaviour has been bad. Employers often lack vital information at difficult times: the fact that you are completely distracted from work because your wife has left you, for instance. People who admit failings and genuinely want to improve will often make the disciplinary panel feel sympathetic. 'The main aim' of disciplinary hearings, as laid down in the Advisory, Conciliation and Arbitration Service (ACAS) code 'is to encourage an employee whose standard of work or conduct is unsatisfactory to improve'.

Negotiate with your employers over your reference if they decide to sack you. Many companies don't want the unpleasantness of giving bad references either. But if you forget to sort out this issue, your career could be blighted for a long time. Free or inexpensive leaflets on discipline are available from ACAS on 01455-852 225.

• •
How to deal with grievance proceedings

Understand that there are two main triggers of the grievance system: a dispute with another colleague or dissatisfaction with a management decision.

Resist, as far as you can, going down this formal route simply because someone gets on your nerves. 'These proceedings are very stressful for everyone,' says employment lawyer Paul Nicholls of Dibb Lupton Alsop. 'You should ask yourself, "Is there another way I can resolve this informally? Is there someone else I can approach in confidence?"' You will find it hard to work with that person again. They will never trust you – and colleagues who might even sympathise with your position could see you as breaking ranks.

Save your fire for the really serious issues. BIFU, the banking union, has seen an increase in grievance proceedings over allegedly unfair annual appraisals, where employees lose out on pay rises after their boss marks them down. 'A rash of grievances being lodged' encouraged Midland Bank managers to stop docking points for staff with 'above average sickness'. 'Using the grievance system can be the only way to sort out a bad appraisal,' says BIFU organiser Richard Lynch.

Work out beforehand how you want the situation resolved. No one will respect you if you are just there to whinge. A grievance is an opportunity to negotiate: you might want more training, to move your desk somewhere less dangerous, to reshuffle your responsibilities. 'Decide on your optimum solution – and then have a fallback position,' advises Lynch.

Don't ever rely on your judgement alone. Have a confidant who will give you objective criticism (not your mother if she always takes your side). Despite the potential cost savings, lawyers rarely represent themselves or their nearest or dearest because they know their outlook is biased. Get someone to accompany you. The government accepts this is useful, hence its decision to allow people to request the presence of a union rep or a colleague.

Prepare your case in detail by writing it down. In the heat of the moment, you may forget your most salient points.

Think again if you have an informal chat with a boss who doesn't respond. 'If someone makes a complaint and nothing is done, disaster ensues,' says Nicholls. 'Companies must tell the person who raises the complaint what is being done.' Perhaps you can speak to someone else – another manager or a personnel officer. Perhaps disaster will ensue if you work in a badly managed business. Keep notes, and decide how you will respond when the post-mortem takes place.

Find out about other procedures for specific complaints if you work in a large organisation with various complaints mechanisms. Firms are so terrified of sexual harrassment and bullying claims that many have established separate arrangements for these allegations.

Holidays

....
How to tell whether you get enough holiday

1 Understand that good employers are increasingly aware of the need to give good holidays. Many are raising their entitlements substantially. Under EU laws, a minimum of four weeks' leave a year is rising to five weeks in 1999. Until this legislation came in, there was no legal right in the UK to paid holiday, and millions of low-paid, part-time workers got nothing. Expect even more if you work in certain industries, according to Incomes Data Services' (IDS) *Hours and Holidays* surveys of leading organisations: the best sector is publishing, with an average in 1997 of 25.6 days; the worst is finance, with 20.9.

2 Don't expect a lower entitlement just because you are a blue-collar worker. There is little difference between holiday levels: about 55 per cent of both white- and blue-collar workers get at least 25 days a year from major employers. But manufacturing companies are more prone to shutting factories at Christmas and other times, and forcing staff to use up holiday then.

Expect to get additional service-related holidays in about half of large companies, according to IDS. 'Virtually all companies in the finance and retail and distribution sectors have service entitlement,' says the report. Many employers give an additional day or two after five, 10, 15 or 20 years' service. In some companies, extra leave is given for rank instead.

Recognise that you are in a weaker bargaining position if you are a casual, temporary or contract worker. Although some senior bank staff get 30 days' holiday, the bank union BIFU is concerned about the growing number of casual workers. 'If you are a casual worker, you usually don't get any holiday,' says a BIFU spokesman. The EU legislation will not improve the position of all workers. Employment solicitor Michael Burd of Lewis Silkin says, 'There will be ways round this for short-term workers. Some people will be so frightened of losing their jobs that they won't take up their rights.'

Take a long weekend or a short break at least once every three months, says stress specialist Professor Cary Cooper of the University of Manchester Institute of Science and Technology (UMIST). 'If you're constantly feeling tired, you look exhausted or you are getting lots of minor ailments, you need a break,' he says. 'Given the pace of life, we probably need more holidays than we ever did.' The 'Defeat Depression' campaign has highlighted insufficient holiday as a cause of stress-linked health problems ranging from anxiety and high blood-pressure to ulcers and heart attacks.

Expect holiday entitlements to rise slightly over the next few years, as EU practices converge. Many German, Italian, Dutch and French workers get more than their UK counterparts – at least six weeks a year.

How to return to work after a holiday

Grieve in private. Civil Servants used to moan aloud about the end of their holidays – but only in the days when they thought they had jobs for life. If you demonstrate the depth of your *Angst* nowadays, you may find yourself on another long holiday. Appreciate that at least you have a job to go back to.

Remember that it is often a good sign if you are sad to be back. If you have been following Transport Minister Glenda Jackson's example, campaigning during her 1996 holiday on the beaches in Benidorm, there is probably something missing from your life.

Keep your holiday snaps to yourself. Once your colleagues see you in a bikini or swimming trunks, you will lose all *gravitas*. If you have a tan and look healthy, that will be provocation enough. Val Tyler of the Industrial Society says, 'If they've all had their noses to the grindstone, it doesn't help if you're going on about just how wonderful the Seychelles were.'

4 **Understand** that you will probably take at least two or three days to return in spirit as well as body. 'Regard it as a decompression chamber,' says former administrator Eoin Kent. 'Do the most attractive kind of work you can.' Val Tyler suggests shock therapy for people who cannot afford a few sluggish days: 'Schedule some pretty tough meetings so that you don't drift off.'

5 **Treat** your colleagues particularly kindly. They all know that they can survive without you, but you have to rely on them to find out what happened while you were away.

6 **Improve** relations with people you don't like. If you haven't seen them for two weeks, you might be able to stomach speaking to them for a few minutes and even asking them how *their* holiday was. Similarly, with a fresh and relaxed eye you may be able to solve some of those problems that previously you thought intractable.

How to cope with a holiday if you are a workaholic

1 **Understand** that you will probably suffer withdrawal symptoms if you are stressed or have become a workaholic. Many people in these categories suffer anxiety, depression and a cough or a cold at the start of a break.

2 **Make** the transition from work less painful by thinking ahead. If you learn a few words of Italian before going to Italy you will be less likely to feel uprooted and wishing you were back at your desk. Decide some of the things you will do on holiday before you go. Have something to look forward to.

3 Abandon your briefcase. Occupational psychologist Sandi Mann of Salford University says it is 'crucial' to take a complete break: 'If you've got work with you, you will always have a reason to feel guilty.'

4 Ration your workload, however, if your addiction is such that you cannot leave it behind. Family or friends have every reason to be upset if you take your mobile phone and laptop PC to the beach. Restrict your work to two hours in the morning or reading the report that has been in your in-tray for weeks. Pansy, an experienced workaholic, says, 'It's a matter of accepting that a well-rested brain works 10 times better than an unrested one. Avoid fiddly detail. You're OK so long as you're dealing in fat thoughts, not thin thoughts.'

5 Set yourself goals on holiday if you are a compulsive achiever. Emulate Captain Mainwaring from *Dad's Army*, who learnt to play the bagpipes on honeymoon.

6 Avoid taking *War and Peace*, and other large, serious volumes, unless you are a genuine highbrow. A workaholic needs to have more fun. These may be wonderful books, but most people will be better off with something lighter.

7 **Don't** cancel your holiday because of work and don't come back early – unless you are the Prime Minister or the situation is desperate. Try to get away from home: a physically different perspective is more stimulating.

8 **Put** greater emphasis on holidays generally. 'Arrange your work around your holidays, not your holidays around your work,' say psychologists Cary Cooper and Susan Cartwright in *Managing Workplace Stress*. Book well in advance and try to take a few long weekends and shorter breaks as well. Plan the next one when you have finished the last: always have something to look forward to.

Redundancy, being sacked ... and starting again

··

How to tell it's time to change jobs

1 Don't wait for the worst signs: your boss rarely looking at you any more; not being invited to meetings; no longer hearing office gossip. 'Being put on "special projects" is usually the kiss of death,' says Catherine Gilbert of outplacement consultancy DBM. 'It means your old role has disappeared.'

2 Remember that it is usually far easier to get a job when you already have one. You will be more confident, won't have to explain what you have been doing since you lost your job, and your financial position will be easier.

3 Consider changing jobs even when you are at your peak. Footballer Eric Cantona would probably have found it more difficult to develop his other interests if he had stayed another season at Manchester United and gone gradually downhill. Similarly, former Chancellor Ken Clarke recognised that he needed to get his new roles sorted out quickly – joining the board of Nottingham Forest FC, for instance – when the Conservatives lost the 1997 general election. If he had simply rested on the back-benches for a couple of years, his cachet would have declined as people started to forget his achievements as chancellor.

4 **Avoid** doing the same job for more than two or three years. 'You've probably learnt all you can in that period,' says Gilbert. If you don't get promotion or take on new responsibilities, you could be regarded as lacking in initiative and unattractive to other employers.

5 **Recognise** that you are particularly vulnerable if you have been with the same company for more than 10 years – even if your role within it has changed. 'You could be labelled complacent,' says Jo Bond of Coutts Career Consultants. 'For someone in their twenties, that might apply after five years.' You will have difficulty proving you can adapt to new environments.

6 **Don't** take heart from the fact that your boss worked in your company man and boy. Even old-fashioned sectors such as insurance now expect many people outside the boardroom to have experience in other companies.

7 **Understand** that you improve your position by learning new skills and maintaining your enthusiasm. Consultant John Floush specialises in advising the over-fifties, and has seen people regain confidence by learning computer and public-speaking skills. But, he says, 'Lots of people of that age just keep their head below the parapet.'

8 **Always** have contingency plans. 'Assume your job is going to come to an end every four or five years – and network like crazy,' says Malcolm Kerrell of the Wildfire consultancy. Work out what you would do next week if you lost your job tomorrow. 'Everyone should be keeping in touch with their jobs marketplace – reading the ads, staying in contact with the agencies, even going for interviews,' says Bond. Everyone should expect to be made redundant once or twice in their career. The more you plan for it, the less likely it is to happen.

. . . .

How to cope with job insecurity

1 **Don't** lie awake at night worrying about what you'll do when you lose your job. Most employees, particularly those over 30, tend to regard themselves as an appendage of their employers and don't do enough to gain some independence. Karen feels too depressed and frightened to look for another job, even though she thinks her bosses are planning to sack her: 'It's a horrible feeling, and I know I'm avoiding taking responsibility. If I find another job now, I might wonder if I've made the right choice. If I wait till I get kicked out, I'll know then that I have no alternative but to get another one.'

2 **Avoid** the short-term solution of ingratiating yourself by faking hard work. Pretenders often get found out if their boss is fired and replaced by a fresh pair of eyes. Unless you gain more genuine self-confidence, you will continue to feel insecure and agitated.

3 **Work** out contingency plans, whether or not you think you might lose your job. Jo Bond of Coutts Career Consultants advises people to keep on updating their CV and going for job interviews. Your confidence could improve dramatically, and you will discover what your weaknesses are. If, for instance, you have worked in the same company for many years, your dress could be outdated. Bond says, 'You might have adopted the corporate appearance of that company – the white shirts of many consultancies or the traditional dress of academics. In the outside world, you could be perceived as a 70s or 80s person, yesterday's man or woman.'

4 **Develop** contacts with people outside your company, urges Paul Le Druillenec, an accountant who has three times found 'life after death' when he was made redundant: 'Every piece of work I've had in the last 20 years has come through contacts of one kind or another.' You'll have to work particularly hard at this if you are a shy, inarticulate backroom person, but you will get better with practice. Join the local Chamber of Commerce, become active in your union, write articles in the trade magazine, go on training courses, ask questions at conferences (it's not so bad after you've done it once), and try to get involved in training other people and doing presentations. Le Druillenec says that many jobs are filled when someone in a company announces: 'We need someone to do *x*. Did you read Joe's article in the journal? Did you hear what Jane said at the conference?'

5 **Organise** your finances to cater for some periods of rest. You will lie awake worrying about the mortgage if you know you are tied in to it for five years and could lose your job tomorrow. Get a loan that doesn't have large penalty clauses for early redemption, and build up some savings.

How to tell if you are about to be fired

1 **Observe** the appearance and bearing of your chief executive. Most get depressed at the thought of laying off staff. (Some, of course, get a spring in their step at the prospect of exercising power.)

2 **Monitor** the movements of the personnel and accounts departments. 'Notice if they have been working late behind closed doors,' says Sam Palmer (not his real name), a manager who has been both executioner and victim. 'Long budget discussions are a bad sign. If your company works on a calendar year, the budget is probably discussed in September and finalised in October.'

3 **Notice** if a senior person in your department leaves in unexpected circumstances. Destabilisation is often the precursor to redundancies. Making people unhappy is seen as a cheap way of getting rid of them in some organisations.

4 **Beware** should rival companies start laying off staff.

5 **Watch** out if senior management begin talking about 'competitive pressures' and the need to improve productivity.

6 **Start** to worry if you don't have enough work to do or the amount of work for your department is cut back.

7 **Get** worried if new people are brought in to manage your company or it is taken over. Bosses find it a lot easier to get rid of strangers than of friends. 'You know you're in trouble,' says Palmer, 'if you see the arrival of a new stock of P45s.' More than 2 million people, nearly one in 10 employees, have been made redundant in the last couple of years.

How to avoid being fired

1 **Avoid** coming in late in the mornings and taking days off sick. These are the kind of criteria employers will use when selecting people for redundancy. Jo Bond of Coutts Career Consultants says, 'Keep fit and healthy. The older you are, the more important it is to project a fit and healthy outlook: it's highly important for people over 40.'

2 **Accept** that redundancy selection is unpleasant and can put you in competition with your peers and friends. The people most likely to survive are those who can prove (whether true or not) that they do a better job than others. If you make more sales than your colleagues, your employers will find it difficult to sack you.

3 **Try** to change your job informally if you think it is becoming redundant. Secretaries who stick to their job description can rapidly find themselves becoming out of date. But if you change with the times – learning IT skills, for example – you are less likely to find yourself being pushed out.

4 **Remember** that many employers use redundancy as an excuse to get rid of people they regard as troublemakers. If you are seen as a free thinker, you may have to be doubly good to keep your job. Elaine Aarons, employment solicitor at Eversheds, advises, 'Keep a distance from the politics in the organisation. It doesn't do someone any good to be going to official or unofficial union meetings. Those people often don't do well when a redundancy selection is going on. Unfortunately, it is as if we are going back into the Dark Ages where employees have to take everything on the chin.'

5 **Network** with other departments. If your skills are appreciated in other parts of the organisation, you are more likely to get the offer of a transfer if your job is made redundant.

6 **Recognise** that you will probably be made redundant at some stage: 10 per cent of the workforce have been so in the last couple of years. To minimise the possibility of redundancy long term, you need to keep brushing up your skills so you can jump ship, if necessary. Remember, there are fewer jobs for generals than for footsoldiers.

•••

How to network

1 **Remember** that networking is becoming increasingly important for people who want to stay in work, particularly among those who are disadvantaged in the jobs market by being older or unemployed. Besides, it works: outplacement consultants say that 50 per cent of clients find jobs this way.

2 **Telephone** useful contacts if you are looking for work and ask to meet them for 30 minutes. Always ask for their 'help and advice', but never ask outright for a job. 'They get embarrassed if you do that,' says Malcolm Kerrell of outplacement consultancy Wildfire Corporation. 'And if they're embarrassed, they won't return your calls.'

3 **Don't** worry about calling people you don't know, but it is far better if you can say that a contact of theirs suggested you ring. If you have a sensible patter and serious questions to ask, many people will co-operate. 'It's subconscious flattery,' says Paul Armstrong of another consultancy, Sanders & Sidley. 'Many of the people you ask for help may be asking *you* for advice in six months.'

December is a good time because many others will, incorrectly, assume that Christmas is a bad time for job-seeking and will leave the field fairly clear.

4 **Stay** in touch with people you meet. Write a letter or phone to thank them for their time, and let them know when you get another job.

5 **Don't** neglect your contacts just because you are in work. Kerrell suggests drawing up a list of people who are important to you – your boss, colleagues, clients, suppliers – and making sure you maintain regular contact with them.

6 **Join** trade associations, alumni clubs and unions. Stay in touch with people you used to work with. Networking can be a cynical exercise – people drop each other when they cease to be useful – but it works best for those who genuinely care for their friends. Researcher Naomi Driver sends out more than 100 Christmas cards to former colleagues and people she met through work: 'I talk to people for their own sake, not because they are important. You get relationships that actually matter, which produces a very strong support network.'

7 **Don't** rely on promises. Some people are so keen to help they make promises they cannot deliver. Others make none, but will work quietly on your behalf.

How to respond if you are offered redundancy

1 Understand the strength of your negotiating position. Your employers will not want to spend months fighting an industrial tribunal case. In many instances, employers are prepared to pay you to go away quietly. You have more room for manoeuvre if you are one of a few employees getting the sack; if hundreds are going, your employers will fight harder against setting a precedent that will raise costs.

2 Don't mention any hopes of getting another job soon. If so, your employer may feel less of an obligation to compensate you.

3 Make sure that you receive your accrued holiday entitlement.

4 Negotiate any benefits you get at work, particularly company cars and health cover. 'It is often very cheap for the employer to continue providing these benefits for a while,' says employment solicitor James Davies of Lewis Silkin.

5 Give reasons why your pay-off should be increased. You could drop the hint of an industrial tribunal claim. Employers are often nervous about bad publicity, and the cost of legal fees and management time. You could give moral arguments, such as length of service and proven loyalty. Surprisingly enough, the moral approach often works.

6 **Ensure** that your package is structured tax-efficiently. The Inland Revenue is increasingly trying to tax redundancy payments, and some employers are not putting up much of a fight. Personnel departments are not tax specialists, so deal with your company's tax specialist, consult your trade union or get professional advice (ask your company to reimburse you).

7 **Insist** on a good reference even if you leave on bad terms. It is preferable to have your departure described as redundancy, not resignation or a euphemistic 'parting of the ways'.

8 **Force** yourself to take these steps, even if it feels alien to your nature. Men, by the by, are twice as likely as women to be made redundant, according to the *Employment Gazette*.

• •

How to be made redundant

1 **Evaluate** your position: if you are underpaid, over-worked, talented and in your twenties you are probably a valuable commodity to your employer. The older you get and the more pay rises you accumulate, the higher your chances of redundancy, says Richard Lynch of banking union BIFU: 'They want to get rid of the old expensive ones and drag in a kid who may be persuaded to do the job on a lower grade and who will certainly be cheaper.'

2 **Work** out what you will do afterwards. Many white-collar staff have ended up in severe financial difficulties because they thought that £30,000 redundancy would last a long time. Visit employment agencies, explore the freelance market and plan exactly how you will earn your living.

3 **Never** suggest to your employer that you are likely to leave anyway. You could say something like, 'The industry has changed a lot since I joined, and I don't feel so enthusiastic any more.' But if you go too far – 'I can no longer perform my duties' – you set yourself up for disciplinary proceedings, whereby a heartless employer could get rid of you at no cost.

4 **Write** a letter outlining your reasons. A tug at the heart-strings is often useful – such as having an aged relative to care for. Make sure the letter goes to people with influence. Your immediate boss might be pleased to see the back of you, but may not know how to achieve this. Write to Personnel, with copies to the area manager, for instance, and your immediate superiors.

5 **Listen** to all office gossip and rumours, and cultivate the finance department. Some industries are constantly looking for cuts, and many department heads are under pressure to reduce budgets. Bernie Corbett of the National Union of Journalists says, 'A journalist's salary will come out of a particular department's budget – but it is likely that a separate budget will be set up for redundancy costs.'

6 **Make** it easy for your employers to get rid of you. Look for a swap, advises BIFU, if your employer is making several people redundant. In the late 1990s, the Midland Bank announced redundancies in Enfield. Many people who did not want to lose their jobs were able to swap with those who wanted to go. The bank's main aim was to get the headcount down rather than to lose particular employees. But the individuals had to take the initiative and give Personnel the name of the person they could switch with. 'If you can do Personnel's job for them, it helps,' says Lynch.

7 **Conceal** your usual enthusiasm if you know that a redundancy selection procedure is going to take place. Companies try to get rid of the poorer performers and will look at absenteeism, skills, disciplinary records, annual appraisals and other indicators.

8 **Accept** that you are unlikely to get a generous pay-off in a small company. Individual sectors can suddenly get tougher in their attitude. Teachers in their fifties used to find it relatively easy to get early retirement – including handsome pension enhancements worth more than £35,000 – but few local authorities can afford them now. Whatever sector you work in, be patient. Many people looking for redundancy will be told that they are too late, have applied in the wrong way and have no chance – then suddenly they are given an offer. 'The trick is persistence,' says Lynch.

How to cope with losing your job

1 **Research** your position, if possible before you become unemployed, by going to your union, a TUC Unemployed Centre, the CAB or a welfare rights centre. 'An awful lot can go wrong,' says Richard Exell of the TUC. Many early retirers are shocked to discover their benefits stop after six months because they draw a pension. They could have improved their position if they had planned.

2 **Sign** on immediately – even if you have a fat redundancy cheque – and keep on signing. Ring the local Job Centre on or before your first day off work to arrange a meeting. You lose state pension and other benefit entitlements if you don't.

3 **Get** advice about the Jobseekers Allowance before your Job Centre interview. You will be asked about preferred jobs and pay levels, and your job-hunting strategy. You can say that you want your last salary level. But, warns GMB benefits researcher Dolores O'Donoghue, 'Don't say that you will take anything.' Job Centres are already very willing to send teachers for jobs as bingo callers. Information about benefits is available in libraries and Job Centres.

4 **'Don't** make long-term investment decisions,' says financial adviser Peter Smith of Hill Martin. Pay off credit-card debts from your redundancy money but remember that you could need to live off the cash for several months.

The Jobseekers Allowance is means-tested after the first six months, and the DSS will not make payments if you have spent the money. Speak to your mortgage lender if you are worried about meeting the payments. 'Building societies are very sympathetic if they are contacted straightaway,' says Kevin Coyne, a former adviser at the Merseyside TUC Unemployed Centre.

5 Prepare for a fall in morale. 'It shocked me to see how rapidly downhill I went,' says Lorna, who was unemployed for three months. 'Going to the gym saved my sanity. I felt I had done something undeniably positive each day.'

6 Expect several weeks of job-hunting: 50 per cent of people take more than six months. Consider going freelance – particularly if you are a professional and over 40. One in seven redundant executives becomes self-employed, according to consultant DBM.

7 Spread the word that you are on the market again. About half of those who go to outplacement consultants find work through personal contacts. Complain privately to friends if you think you were badly treated by your old bosses: frustrations can come through in formal job interviews and put off potential employers.

How to go freelance

1 **Don't** assume that you are suited to the insecurities of being a lone ranger. Gregarious, outgoing people often wilt when left alone. Outplacement consultant Sanders & Sidley find that 40 per cent of people who initially opt to go freelance subsequently change their minds. Managing director Frances Cook says the necessary qualities for freelances include 'tenacity, resilience, self-motivation, discipline, good financial management and regarding new things as a challenge'.

2 **Make** the change gradually if you can. Build up some freelance work while you are still employed. This way you can test the market and your own psychology, as well as strengthening your self-confidence, before you take the plunge. 'Try to have a contract to start off with – ideally someone agreeing to pay you a certain amount a month,' says self-employed accountant Paul Le Druillenec. Don't rely on kind words: the most vociferous promisors of commissions are often the ones who let you down.

3 **Build** up a range of customers – at least five, but perhaps many more, suggests Sanders & Sidley. If you are reliant on just one or two companies, you are always at their mercy. If there is a change in personnel, you can find your workload drying up overnight.

4 **Set** aside a given amount of time – between 9.00 and 10.00 am each day, perhaps – to do your marketing and selling. There is no point in being brilliant at your job unless you can sell your wares. Invoice promptly and negotiate over fees. Even the nicest people will take advantage of you if you don't fight your corner. However, if you can't bear discussing money, get a partner, accountant or business-manager figure to do it for you. But keep a sharp eye on them: it's not only young, talented pop stars who are worked over by their minders.

5 Avoid the temptation to become a workaholic. If you get a good reputation, you could be inundated with offers. Because every day means money, some freelances stop taking holidays or weekends. 'This can be bad for you,' says psychologist Michael Carroll of consultancy Right Cavendish. 'The quality of your work can suffer, since there is no one around to tell you that you are working too hard.'

6 Recognise that the rest of your life will need to change because of this dramatic overhaul of your working environment. You may need to socialise more in the evenings if you spend a lot of time working alone.

7 Take out a mortgage or any loans you need *before* you go freelance – but only if you are confident that you can maintain the payments. It is far more difficult to get a loan when you are not on a payroll. You often need to produce three years of accounts, for example.

How to find a job at 50

1 Accept that it will be difficult. Some employers are ageist, and may even have decided to cut down on future pension costs by avoiding older employees. But you are most likely to get a job if you do not allow yourself to get demoralised.

2 Bring your skills up to date. Some temporary agencies provide free training. Many higher education institutions run night courses at cheap rates.

3 Meet as many people as you can. This will raise your spirits, enable you to learn from the experiences of others and help you to find jobs through networking. Tell your existing contacts that you are looking for a job, go on training courses, visit information centres such as libraries and the local Job Club.

4 Re-evaluate your talents. Lilian Bennett, the chair of Manpower, says: 'Older people sometimes don't recognise that they don't have the distraction that a young family can bring. They have a different and better work ethic. And they have experience. Women returning to work after bringing up a family may not recognise that they now have experience of budgeting, training and administration, and that they have a number of extra things to offer employers.'

5 Don't apologise for your age. This will not improve your chances with people who are prejudiced and could make you appear hangdog in front of the others. You might want to bring your wardrobe up to date, however.

6 Consider a career change. Law firms may be biased against taking on a 55-year-old solicitor, but your local college may want to find a part-time law lecturer with practical experience.

7 Get the books and booklets. The Department for Education and Employment will send a free copy of its booklet *Too Old – Who Says?* to people who write to Camberstown Ltd, Unit 8, Goldthorpe Industrial Estate, Goldthorpe, Rotherham, South Yorkshire, S63 9BL. Piatkus Books (0171-631 0710) publishes *Jobs for the Over 50s – How to find work which values your experience* by Linda Greenbury (£8.99). If you are looking for office work in the London area, you can also contact the specialist recruitment agency *Forties People* on 0171-329 4044.

8 Cheer yourself up with the reflection that ageism at work will probably be tackled at some stage by legislation. The government is increasingly aware that people need to carry on working for longer in their lives (but usually in a part-time job) because we are simply living longer. Experts predict that many countries around the world will soon raise the retirement age to 70 – and will then have to force employers to take on older workers.

How to prepare for retirement

1 **Recognise** that retirement can come as a major shock unless you plan well ahead. Workaholics suffer most. Sociologist Professor Alan Walker of Sheffield University says, 'It is quite common for people to experience a psychological decline and depression after losing a very active role. It is crucial that they find an alternative source of stimulation.' After 40 years of carrying responsibility, making decisions and meeting deadlines, you will probably feel flat spending your time watching television.

2 **Talk** through your all options with spouse, friends or family, advises the charity Age Concern. Even the best relationships can come under strain when you are suddenly together for all the time you used to spend at work and travelling there – typically about 50 hours a week in total. 'Some people find it quite threatening to have all this time,' says an Age Concern spokeswoman. 'The financial issues are also huge. Housing is very important: many people decide to live somewhere else.'

3 **Attend** any pre-retirement seminars run by your company. Some employers give very useful benefits of this kind – week-long courses, advice on finding part-time work, for example, or access to library and telephones for a few months after you retire. Read some of the numerous books on this issue – Age Concern's *The Retirement Guide* (£7.99), for instance, or Rosemary Brown's *Your Retirement* (Kogan Page, £8.99).

4 **Understand** that you can probably extend your lifespan by developing your range of activities. 'People who have interests outside themselves have the best overall health and sense of well-being,' says the Age Concern spokeswoman. US gerontologist Robert Butler has found a correlation between health and activity. Dr David Weeks and Jamie James say in their book *Superyoung – the proven way to stay young forever*, 'The superyoung view retirement as practically meaningless, for it in no way signifies a retreat from or a diminished commitment to the concerns that absorbed them previously. It's not a time for disengagement in any form . . . For the superyoung, retirement is a time for self-discovery and reviewing one's life, especially for those who had little time to contemplate such personal issues in the past.'

5 **Increase** the amounts you put into your pension if you are still a little way off retiring. Most pensioners are shocked to find how little they have to spend. Only 28 per cent of retired people have more than £150 a week to live off.

Useful addresses and telephone numbers

Advisory, Conciliation and Arbitration Service (ACAS)

Brandon House
180 Borough High Street
London
SE1 1LW

See in local directories for local numbers or call
℡ 0171-210 3613

Age Concern

Astral House
1268 London Road
London
SW16 4ER

℡ 0181-679 8000

Alcohol Concern

Waterbridge House
323–36 Loman Street
London
SE1 0EE   ℘ 0171-928 7377

Apex Trust *helping ex-prisoners gain employment*

St Alphage House
2 Fore Street
London
EC2Y 5DA   ℘ 0171-638 5931

Association of Relocation Agents

Premier House
11 Marlborough Place
Brighton
East Sussex
BN1 1UB   ℘ 01273 624455

Commission for Racial Equality

Headquarters Office
Elliott House
10–12 Allington Street
London
SW1 5EH   ℘ 0171-828 7022

Cruse *bereavement counselling*

Cruse House
126 Sheen Road
Richmond
Surrey
TW9 1UR ℘ 0181-940 4818

Disability Alliance

Universal House
88–94 Wentworth Street
London
E1 7SA ℘ 0171-247 8776

Equal Opportunities Commission

Overseas House
Quay Street
Manchester
M3 3HN ℘ 0161-833 9244

European Commission *UK office*

8 Storey's Gate
London
SW1P 3AT ℘ 0171-973 1992

Health and Safety Commission and Executive

Rose Court
2 Southwark Bridge
London
SW1P 2HW   ✆ 0171-717 6000

House of Commons

Westminster
London
SW1A OPW   ✆ 0171-219 3000

Industrial Society

48 Bryanston Square
London
W1H 7LN   ✆ 0171-479 2000)

Institute of Personnel and Development

IPD House
Camp Road
London
SW19 4UX   ✆ 0181-971 9000

Mind *hotline – information line on mental health issues*

✆ 0345 660163

Nacro *National Association for the Care and Resettlement of Offenders*

169 Clapham Road
London
SW9 OPU $\emptyset$ 0171-582 6500

National Union of Students

461 Holloway Road
London
N7 6LJ $\emptyset$ 0171-272 8900

Occupational Pensions Regulatory Authority

Invicta House
Trafalgar Place
Brighton
East Sussex
BN1 4DW $\emptyset$ 01273 627600

Pension Schemes Registry

c/o OPRA
PO Box 1NN
Newcastle-upon-Tyne
NE99 1NN $\emptyset$ 0191-225 6393

Public Concern at Work

Suite 306
16 Baldwins Gardens
London
EC1N 7RJ   ✆ 0171-404 6609)

The Samaritans

✆ 0345 909090

Trades Union Congress

Congress House
Great Russell Street
London
WC1B 3LS   ✆ 0171-636 4030

Vacation Work Publications

9 Park End Street
Oxford
OX1 1HJ   ✆ 01865 241978